how to get a

PAY

RISE

how to get a

PAY

ROS JAY

RISE

a bonus, or promotion,

or whatever else you want

an imprint of Pearson Education

London • New York • San Francisco • Toronto • Sydney • Tokyo • Singapore
Hong Kong • Cape Town • Madrid • Paris • Milan • Munich • Amsterdam

PEARSON EDUCATION LIMITED

Head Office:
Edinburgh Gate
Harlow CM20 2JE
Tel: +44 (0)1279 623623
Fax: +44 (0)1279 431059

London Office:
128 Long Acre
London WC2E 9AN
Tel: +44 (0)20 7447 2000
Fax: +44 (0)20 7240 5771
Website: www.business-minds.com

First published in Great Britain in 2001

ISBN 0 273 65483 7

British Library Cataloguing in Publication Data
A CIP catalogue record for this book can be obtained from the British Library

10 9 8 7 6 5 4 3 2 1

Designed by Claire Brodmann Book Designs, Lichfield, Staffs.
Typeset by Northern Phototypesetting Co. Ltd, Bolton
Printed and bound in Great Britain by Biddles Ltd, *www.biddles.co.uk*

The Publishers' policy is to use paper manufactured from sustainable forests.

About the author

Ros Jay is a freelance business writer and editor. She writes on a range of business topics specialising in marketing and communication-related subjects. She also writes for and edits corporate magazines, both in print and on the net. She is a senior associate of the Institute of Direct Marketing.

Acknowledgements

I would like to thank all the people, including the many HR professionals, who have helped with the material for this book. In particular I would like to thank Carol, Richard Craze and Rachael Stock.

Contents

contents

Introduction

Fancy a pay rise? Course you do. Who doesn't? So how come some people get bigger or more frequent pay rises than the rest of us? There's a very simple reason: they know how to. It isn't that they are luckier than us, or that they have kinder bosses. No. They know that there are two key elements to getting a pay rise, and they have mastered them both:

- Be worth it.
- Know how to ask for it.

That's what this book is all about.

Did you know that three out of four people have never asked for a pay rise? Well, it's not surprising if they never get one, then. Simply making the decision to ask for a pay rise is a big step towards getting it.

Most of us reckon we deserve more than we get paid. And most of us are right. But it's not you that needs to know it, of course. It's your boss. *How to get a pay rise* will show you how to help your boss see the light. Pay rises that motivate people (and that's most pay rises, frankly) improve performance out of all proportion to their cost. That's why Henry Ford said the pay rise was 'the finest cost-cutting move we ever made'. So do your boss a favour. Make it your mission to demonstrate how much they can gain by this simple expedient of upping your salary.

Once you've learnt the trick of getting what you want and deserve from your boss – to your mutual benefit – you can apply it to more than just a pay rise. Maybe you're after a promotion, or a company car, or longer holiday entitlement. No problem. It's all in here: the tips and techniques for helping your organisation motivate you better by showing you what you're really worth to them.

1

HOW TO BE WORTH IT

Obviously you want more than you're getting from your employers in recognition of your value – that's why you're here. Maybe you want a better car (or any car), or longer holidays, or first-class travel for all those train journeys you're expected to make. Perhaps you want a bigger and better office, or to work from home two days a week. Or maybe, dammit, you just want the hard cash in your hand at the end of the month.

All these perks and pay rises are variations on the same theme. You want to feel valued by your employers, and you need them to show you that they really *do* value you. Just as your partner might buy you flowers or treat you to a surprise meal out, you want your employers to show that they love you too. (Only you'll do without the flowers if they'll just stick a zero on the end of your pay cheque.)

All the evidence shows that people who feel appreciated work harder. And not just harder, but better too. We are more productive when we feel loved and happy – it's obvious. We wash the dishes faster when we're cheerful, we fix the car more easily when we're feeling good, we have more fun with the kids when we're relaxed and happy. And we're no different at work from the way we are at home. If it's so obvious to us, why haven't our employers noticed it too?

Well maybe they have. But they can't afford to pay everyone more than they're worth, can they? That would be unprofitable. No, they have two criteria for keeping costs down:

1   They won't up your salary or perks for no reason if they think you're quite happy with what you're getting now.
2   They won't pay employees more than they are worth to the company.

So your job is to show them that they are not meeting either of these two criteria. The first one is pretty easy – you just tell them you're not as happy as they think. We'll find out just how to do that in the second part

people who feel appreciated
work harder

of the book (*How to get what you want*). The important bit for the moment is the second criterion: they won't pay you more than you're worth. Or, to be more specific, more than they *perceive* you are worth.

That's what this first part of the book is all about. Your mission is to show that you are worth more than you're getting. And the greater the difference between your present salary and your true worth, the more you should be asking for. You need to start by assessing what you really *are* worth, and then you can spend time increasing your value before you ask for your pay rise – so you can justify the best pay rise possible.

The information's all in here, but it's up to you. If you reckon you're already worth more than you're being paid, you can ask for it now. Or you can follow the advice in this part to boost your value even more first, and then ask for a more substantial rise. You choose.

Either way, the important thing is to make sure you are worth more than you're getting. Once you can demonstrate that you are being underpaid for the contribution you make to the organisation, your employers will find it very hard to refuse your claim for a rise. If your partner brings more than you could hope for to the relationship or the family, you say thank you to them with treats and gifts (don't you?). Well, it's high time your employers started bringing you roses ...

chapter one

HOW TO ASSESS YOUR VALUE

So what are you worth? Are they paying you enough? Are they paying you too much already? You can't possibly justify a pay rise to your boss if you don't even know yourself whether you're worth it. So the first thing you have to do is to calculate your value to the company.

Of course, you can't assess value in cash terms alone. So you're going to have to check out a wider range of measures than that. There are objective measures:

■ salary benchmark

■ replaceability.

And there are subjective measures:

■ direct value

■ performance

■ team value.

objective measures

The aim here is not to judge your own personal value, but to judge what a person – any competent person – in your job is worth. Is your salary a fair reflection of the value of your job? Does your organisation pay you roughly the same as other employees whose roles are equally valuable? As a press officer, say – or departmental manager, or sales executive, or research scientist or whatever post you hold – are you being paid less than the receptionist, or more than the production director, or the same as a senior sales executive? If you take salaries as a symbol of worth, where on the organisational scale does your job fit in?

salary

The thing you need to assess here is how your pay compares with the going rate for the job. Are you being paid the same as other people in similar positions in your organisation? And what about those outside the organisation? If your employer pays better than the rest of the industry, and you are already earning more than your peers, you're going to have to prove you're better than all the rest to stand any chance of justifying a rise. On the other hand, maybe your employers are poor payers and many of your colleagues earn more than you. That gives you a very good case for a rise from the outset. So benchmark your salary.

'Great. And how do I do that?' (you may be wondering). 'Am I supposed to go round asking everyone else in the company how much they get paid? Or maybe you want me to break into the HR office after closing time and rifle through the personnel files?'

Neither of those, actually. It isn't easy to find out exactly what all your colleagues are getting paid, but it's usually possible to get a fair idea. OK, you might not get a precise figure for every last person, but you can get as much as you need. Here are a few pointers:

- Instead of asking people what *they* are paid, ask them if they know what anyone else is paid. They're much more likely to tell you.

- Do you have any good friends who know what your peers are being paid? A secretary or assistant who will give you information about their boss, or a mate in the HR department? The longer someone has been in the organisation, the more likely they are to know.

- HR departments often keep market survey data. Or simply ask them where you stand in terms of salary across the organisation. They're not likely to give you an exact answer, but they'll usually give you a rough guide. Ask them, 'I have a feeling I'm being undervalued and wondered if you could help me find out if that's true?'

- Good friends and colleagues may be happy to 'show you theirs if you'll show them yours'. Go for it.

- A lot of people may be more prepared to tell you roughly what they earn rather than exactly. It's easier for them to say 'Between £25,000 and £35,000' rather than give you the precise figure. Anything's better than nothing.

■ If you have a colleague (or more than one) who does an almost identical job to you, you may be able to pool your resources. You could both ask for a rise together, along the lines of 'We think this organisation should pay its press officers more'. One word of warning, though: if you reckon your fellow press officer is less valuable than you to the organisation, you may find you've reduced your bargaining leverage. But if they are equally talented, or even more so (as if that were possible), they could help your case.

■ Try to find out what other perks your colleagues have to offset against their salary. Most of these should be obvious – you'll know what company car they have, whether they get to work from home, and so on. But you might not have noticed if they get more holiday entitlement than you, or if they get to stay in better hotels on business trips. All these perks are part of the equation, so use the same methods to elicit this information.

This research needs to strike a balance. Don't give up too easily or you won't be able to build such a strong case. Then again, don't spend months trying to compile a detailed schedule of earnings for everyone in the organisation. You're trying to find out if your own salary is par for the course or not, and assemble enough evidence to be able to justify the answer.

keep it to yourself

Unless you know you can trust a colleague, it's best not to let on that you're planning to ask for a rise (unless you decide a joint request is your best approach). If your boss finds out, they may start preparing their case for the defence. In any case your boss will have only a limited scope for manoeuvre in their budget, and if others are prompted to ask for a rise themselves you may find your share of the resources dwindles.

Right. Next thing. You've established whether your salary is average for the organisation, but is your organisation average for the industry? You might be the top-paid press officer in your company, but if your company pays its press officers well below the national average, you can still justify asking for a rise. So you need to benchmark your salary within the industry as well as the company.

How do you do that? Well, it's not that hard because there's plenty of information out there. You just have to know where to look. So here are some ideas:

- Trade journals and magazines often publish surveys of salaries within the industry. Read them regularly.

- You can write for information to trade publications or trade bodies, who may well be able to point you towards information even if they don't have it themselves.

- Try an internet search. Start with a search engine and key in something like 'salary survey' and the name of your industry. (Make sure you check that the source of the data matches your geographical location as closely as possible – you don't want to benchmark your salary against some third-world country on the other side of the globe.)

- Get the closest industry match you can, but don't expect miracles. For example, if you work for a water company you may be unable to find a survey of salaries among water company staff, but perhaps you can find a survey of utility companies generally.

- Look at recruitment ads in your industry, in the national press, in trade publications and on the net to find out what salaries are offered for posts comparable to yours.

- Talk to headhunters and recruitment agencies and find out what you could expect to earn elsewhere.

- Ask people in other organisations what they earn. They have far less reason to hide the information than your own colleagues do. Maybe you have friends at other companies, or you could talk to people on other exhibition stands at trade fairs. Swap them information about your salary and perks. By the way, it's a lot less pushy to say 'What does your organisation pay press officers?' rather than 'How much do you earn?'

back your case up with hard facts
if you possibly can

By the time you've finished this process, you should be clear about how your own salary fits in with your own organisation, and with the wider industry. Already that tells you whether you're getting a good rate for the job or a bad one.

replaceability

Like the salary research you've just done, this is another objective measure. The question you need to answer is this: how easily could this organisation find another person to fill my post competently? We'll be looking at the subjective side of this later on – whether any replacement could possibly perform as well as you – but at this stage we're considering market forces. Is the market flooded with experienced people looking for work as press officers, or are they impossible to find? It's going to be an important factor to your boss in deciding what you're worth, so you need to have the facts at your fingertips.

Again, you may well glean valuable information from trade publications and from recruitment organisations. Presumably you know roughly whether your sort are ten a penny or whether you're gold dust, but back your case up with hard facts if you possibly can. If you know the average number of qualified applicants per vacancy in your field, you've got a good guide to your replaceability.

furnish facts

Never lose sight of your boss's point of view. If they give you a rise, they'll have to justify it to *their* boss. So encourage them by making it easy for them. Find hard facts for them to use: 'According to a survey by so-and-so, eight out of ten PR managers said they had trouble finding experienced press officers'... that sort of thing.

The fact is – unfair though it may seem – your value is largely determined by this kind of impersonal factor which takes no account of your individual merits. But forewarned is forearmed. If you can establish that there are thousands of eager and skilled people out there ready to step into your shoes, at least you know how much work you have to do to show your boss that you're worth ten of any one of them.

So those are the two objective guides to your value that you need to establish: are you already being paid a fair wage for the job, and how easy is it to find someone else who can fill your post?

subjective measures

direct value

Now this is a really useful guide to how much you're worth. By direct value, I mean how much money do you generate for your organisation? I think the drawback here is obvious, namely how on earth do you know? If you're very lucky, you'll do a job that makes it clear. If you're a sales executive and you bring in £100,000 worth of sales a year, that's your answer. But if you're not a sales executive, that doesn't help a lot.

Very few people are in a position to give a simple, clear answer to the question of their direct value. Now, I have to tell you that in a lot of jobs this is going to be next to impossible to establish. But I'm including it in your overall assessment of your worth because if you *can* work it out, you'll be doing yourself a big favour. In fact, you don't necessarily need to put a final and complete figure on it. You need only demonstrate – if you can – that you generate comfortably more income than you cost the company.

If you actually are generating direct sales, you won't need my help working out how much business you bring in to the organisation. But here are some examples of the kind of income – or savings – you can demonstrate even if you work in accounts, PR, production or distribution.

11

you don't only have to bring in sales to generate wealth

- Orders placed as a result of a marketing, sales or PR campaign that you were responsible for.
- Increased productivity due to a new system you proposed.
- Savings generated because you devised a more streamlined procedure.

You see, you don't only have to bring in sales to generate wealth. You can indirectly boost sales, you can increase effectiveness and productivity, or you can save money by improving equipment, systems or procedures.

There's one more point to look out for here: any income or savings contribute to your value, but generating significant wealth that is down to you personally is best of all. Any sales person should create income. The critical factor is how much did you generate above the average expected in your job? As a marketing person, you're already being paid to run income-generating campaigns. If you want to be paid more, you need to show that your campaigns generate more than other people's.

performance

Income generated is an important factor, but it's not the only one (luckily, if you don't work in a direct income-generating role). You must have objectives and targets in your job – have you met them, or even exceeded them? If you're being paid a standard rate for the job but your performance is well above standard, you deserve more. Likewise if your standard is below par, I wouldn't advise tempting fate by asking for a pay rise until you've improved your performance.

Objectives and targets are really the key to this. You need to assess how well you have met them in order to establish your value to the organisation in terms of performance. And take into account whether your targets have been set higher or lower than average. It may be that if you have consistently performed well your boss will be setting you more stringent targets than other people. In this case, even if you haven't exceeded them, you may still have outclassed everyone else.

x marks the spot

Write down all the targets you have been set in your job, and mark a tick or a cross beside each according to whether you have met it (or are on target to do so) or not. This gives you a single, clear assessment of which parts of your job you are most successful in, and therefore where you provide your organisation with the most (and least) value for money.

team value

You've assessed your job from an objective point of view, you've assessed how much wealth you generate for the organisation, and you've assessed your overall performance in terms of objectives and targets. But there is one more factor that is going to be important to your boss in deciding whether to give you a rise: your value as a member of the team.

What your boss wants is a team made up of members who work together to create a whole that is greater than the sum of its parts. Are you helping to achieve this? If you get on well with other people (inside and outside your department), are popular, positive and encourage others to perform well, you're valuable. If you have your own team to lead, your boss will want to know that you are fair, well respected and can motivate your own team members.

If, on the other hand, you are negative, discouraging and invite conflict, and you are more fond of finding problems than solutions, your value to the organisation isn't going to be as high. Most of us are moderately good team players, but we generally have the odd weakness or two. What are yours? Are you impatient with younger members of the team? Do you get despondent about projects too easily? Are you prone to argue, or to sulk? Are you inclined to keep things to yourself instead of sharing them with the team? Make an honest assessment of yourself.

assessing your value

If you're serious about getting this rise, you must make an honest and fair assessment of your value in the five key areas we've just highlighted. I suggest you grade yourself in each area out of ten. There's not a lot you can do about the first two, but you still need to know where you stand. For the other three, give yourself marks out of ten and then list your key strengths (to point out to your boss when the time comes) and your chief weaknesses.

find your weaknesses

If you're serious about identifying your weaknesses (and you'll have to be if you want a decent rise), try asking other people. Your best friends in the organisation – or colleagues from past jobs – may be prepared to tell you. Or they might anonymously tell someone else acting on your behalf. Or agree to get together with others and write you an 'anonymous' collective note. (If no one dares point out any weaknesses to you even when you ask, and even if you get them drunk first, that's probably a big clue to your first weakness.)

Now, look. You're going to have to be honest here and I know that isn't always easy. But your boss isn't going to have any trouble listing your weaknesses, so you'd better manage it too. You don't have to tell anyone else but yourself, after all. If you want to maximise your value – which is what the next few chapters are about – you've got to minimise your weaknesses. And you can't do that if you don't know what they are.

If your assessment indicates that you are already worth way more than you're being paid, you may want to go ahead and ask for a rise right now. If that's the case, you can skip on to page 73. But if you want the best possible pay rise (or other recognition of your value), you'd do better to improve on your direct value, performance and team value as much as possible before you ask. The more you're worth, after all, the more you're likely to get. The remaining chapters in this part cover the core skills you need to acquire in order to maximise your value.

summary

So that's your starting point if you're serious about getting this rise or whatever it is you want. Make an honest and fair assessment of your value in the five key areas we've highlighted:

1   salary benchmark

2   replaceability

3   direct value (if there is any way you can demonstrate it)

4   performance

5   team value.

You'll have to be brutally honest with yourself, especially about your weaknesses. List these so that you can work to eradicate them and increase your overall worth. The remaining chapters in this part cover the core skills you need to acquire in order to maximise your value. The aim is to make yourself indispensable. That way, whatever you ask for, your boss won't dare to say no.

chapter two

HOW TO EXPAND YOUR SKILLS

Every job has scope for
learning new skills

You may well have discovered, in assessing your value, that you would be worth more to your employer if you had additional skills. Or maybe if you simply improved on existing skills. I'm talking here about learnable, quantifiable skills that are specific to your job, not general skills that apply to any job (such as time management, team skills and so on). We'll address general skills later in the book, but for now we're concerned with job-specific stuff like:

- becoming quicker and more adept at using the new computer software
- getting an HGV licence
- improving your presentation techniques
- being able to budget
- learning to write press releases
- developing your ability to train new staff
- learning to draw up complex project schedules
- writing sales proposals
- training for a professional qualification
- learning a foreign language.

The list is potentially endless, so I'll stop there. You get the gist. New skills make you more valuable to the organisation, and more valuable people deserve to be paid more, or given more perks and privileges. Every job has scope for learning new skills – skills that enable you to perform better or to relieve the workload on others so that they can perform better. So draw yourself up a list of skills that you could usefully learn – or improve on – and that will benefit your employers.

help out

If you have all the skills you need for your own job honed to perfection (be honest), there is still room to increase your value by learning part of your boss's job. Obviously you don't want to tread on their toes or make them feel that you are after their job (unless they vacate it by being promoted). So choose skills that will save them a task they dislike doing, and won't make them feel threatened. You can ask, for example: 'Would it help you if I learned to deliver some of the induction training? It would free you up to concentrate on more urgent projects' or 'What if I helped you write the sales proposals? Then you could spend more time with customers.'

which skills?

This pay rise thing has a basic component you need to be aware of from the start: there isn't a specific point you have to reach before you ask for a rise. You can ask now if think you're being undervalued at the moment. Or you can spend a couple of months increasing your value and then ask for more than you would right now. Or double your value over the next year or two and then ask. Where does it stop? Should you wait until you're worth a hundred times more and then, a month before you finally retire, ask for the mother of all salary increases?

There is no right or wrong answer to this question. All I can tell you is that if you increase your value by 0.1 per cent each week and ask for a 0.1 per cent rise on a weekly basis, I don't think it will be long before your boss starts getting fed up with you. But if you ask only once every ten years – with a steady increase in value throughout that time – you'll be missing out. And you'll be asking for a massive percentage rise, which may be more than your boss's budget will allow.

aim to get a rise ...
every year

As a very broad rule of thumb, aim to get a rise – or promotion or significant perk – every year, maybe linked to your annual salary review (we'll look at the whole question of timing in detail later on). But to do this, you're going to have to be able to demonstrate a substantial increase in your value every year with new, useful skills and new responsibilities. Being realistic, the more staid organisations, where pay rises are rare and money may be tight, are unlikely to reward you this often (although you can still lobby for a better annual bonus or other forms of recognition). But a forward-thinking, successful company which regularly gives pay rises to worthy employees should be happy to recognise a significant increase in your value on a yearly basis.

All of this makes a difference to which skills you need to develop. If you want to show a significant rise in your value over a year, you can focus your efforts on long-term learning. If you want to boost your worth in the next few months, you might be better off brushing up on three or four skills you can learn more quickly. In deciding which skills to start work on first, you need to balance four factors:

- *Which skills will be the most valuable to the organisation?* There's not much value in brushing up your school French if almost all the company's overseas contacts speak Spanish.

- *How good are you already?* If you're already very good at giving presentations, becoming brilliant isn't going to be worth that much more to your boss – although it may be quick and easy for you to do. Better maybe to focus on improving your atrocious writing skills, or learning to operate useful software you aren't at all familiar with.

■ *Which skills can you master most easily?* You might choose to work on several areas at once. But you don't want to have to learn two new languages, get your head round budgeting and start training for an MBA all at the same time. You've still got your regular job to do after all. You can manage several easy skills simultaneously, but perhaps only one difficult one at a time.

■ *How long will each one take to master?* Again, you might need only a week to learn the new software, whereas it could take two years to get a professional qualification.

You may be lucky enough to have come up with a relatively short list of valuable skills that will take only a few months to perfect. There again, you may not. Maybe there's several years' work there. So where to start? It depends very much on how much value you want to add and how fast. In theory, your best bet is to add to your portfolio the skills that are of most worth to your organisation. But if acquiring these is a long way off, maybe you should balance them with a couple of useful and quicker skills – writing press releases, software training or whatever – so you can demonstrate an increase in your value quite soon.

get the boss on your side

If you're not sure which skills are most valuable, there's a simple solution: ask. Tell your boss you want to add to your skills base, and you'd like to know what would be the most useful skills you could learn or improve on. Once they've told you what would be valuable, they're in no position to argue later when, having acquired the skill, you point out that your value to the organisation has increased.

Your priority list might also be influenced by your current position. If you think you already deserve a salary increase, you can ask for it now. That way, you've got a good year in which to train yourself up to be worth the next rise you ask for. If, on the other hand, you reckon your present salary is about fair but you want to be worth a rise as soon as possible, you probably want to add a good number of new skills you can learn fast, as well as making sure that at least one or two have really substantial value.

how to learn new skills

It's pretty obvious how to learn a lot of skills, but some aren't so obvious. The important thing is to involve your boss. They don't have to know you're planning to ask for a rise, but if they work out that you are it still doesn't matter. They know they won't give it to you unless you're worth it, and if you are they'll be happy to. Their job is simply to make sure that you are worth as much as possible to the organisation.

So if you need any help, ask for it. Here are a few examples:

- 'There's an evening course in Spanish at my local college, but I'd have to leave work at ten to five on a Thursday. Would that be OK?'

- 'I can stay late for a few evenings to learn the new software, but could you arrange for a terminal to be available for me to use?'

- 'Can you enrol me on a course to improve my presentation skills?'

- 'I really want to get my MBA. Could you ask for the company to sponsor me?'

- 'If I enrol on a course to learn Spanish, could I go out to Madrid for the trade show in August? It would be a good time for me to start getting some practice.'

- 'Apparently Sales are running a course on proposal writing. Any chance I could join in?'

Your boss is likely to want to see you putting in some effort to fit your new training around your normal work. Staying late or doing evening courses shows you are really keen to add value to yourself, and that earns you useful brownie points. Equally, if a suitable course is only running during the working day, you'll get further if you offer to work late if need be to catch up lost work.

With your boss's help, you can find a convenient opportunity to learn most skills. However, you may have trouble finding courses and training session on certain skills, or in finding ones that you can fit around your work schedule. If this is the case, you'll find that some skills can be learnt effectively from books (for example, how to get a pay rise), or from tapes, CDs or CD-ROMs (such as language courses), or home study courses.

If you can't find a convenient course but feel you need interactive training, try to identify someone in the organisation who is prepared to train you one to one. This works well for learning systems that are specific to the company, that you won't find an external course for. And it can be the best way to learn other skills too. Here are some ideas:

- Often it is your boss who is the closest-to-hand expert on your chosen subject, and who has a vested interest in you learning it yourself. Maybe they will spend a couple of lunchtimes explaining budgets to you, or showing you how to draw up production schedules.

- Approach the best person you know at performing the skill in question. Go to the organisation's star report writer for coaching in how to brush up your own reports. Most people are flattered to be asked, and will help if you offer them a bottle of wine, or a decent meal out, while they're explaining the rudiments of good writing to you.

- Maybe you could swap skills, perhaps with a close colleague. You might be an acknowledged star when it comes to running training courses. Offer to pass on your best tips to a colleague who finds training tough, in exchange for the secrets of their much praised skill at chairing meetings.

summary

You can add value to yourself by expanding your job-specific skills. The way to do this is:

- List the skills you could usefully learn or brush up on to make yourself more valuable.
- Decide which of these skills you are going to tackle first.
- Enlist your boss's help.
- Find a course, book, CD or home study course, or ask someone in the organisation to train you one to one.

Don't bite off more than you can chew, especially if your boss knows what you're doing. Abandoning your training won't look good, however justified it is. Better to start modestly and add new skills as soon as you feel you can cope with them.

get a life

Keep in mind your objective here. You're trying to secure a decent pay rise, that's all. It's not a life or death thing. Don't make yourself miserable trying to cover eight evening classes a week and then sitting up until three in the morning writing essays for the Open University. Have a life. And if it takes you a little longer to acquire the new skills, that's OK. Go for a smaller rise this time and add a few more skills before the next time you ask for an increase.

The remaining chapters in this part are about general skills rather than job-specific ones. All of them are essential to maximising your value (or we wouldn't bother with them here), but they are worthless without the specific skills you need to do your job. Start with the skills you have just identified, and use the following chapters to use these job skills to maximum effect.

3

chapter three

HOW TO IMPROVE YOUR PERSONAL PROFILE

Who do you reckon are the high fliers among your colleagues? If you were in charge, who would you be giving the pay rises to? Some people just stand out as being valuable employees before you've even considered their specific skills or the wealth they generate for the organisation. It's worth thinking about what gives someone an air of success, because once you know what the ingredients are, you can begin to cultivate them for yourself.

your personal image

The way you come across to other people is an important part of how they assess your value. So it's well worth sprucing up your personal image to let your boss and more senior management see that you are an asset to the organisation. This isn't a matter of trying to turn yourself into someone else – that never works – it's just a case of building on key strengths and minimising weaknesses.

The list below covers the key characteristics that will give you an image of success. The vast majority of us possess many of these already, but we have some areas where there is room for improvement. That's all this is about: making a conscious effort to project the best possible side of ourselves all the time.

Don't expect miracles here. It will take people a while to notice the change, but they will notice it eventually. I have a friend I've known for about 20 years. He was always thoroughly unreliable, arriving ludicrously late – if at all – when invited for a meal or a party. Not long ago I made an arrangement with him and then teased him saying, 'I don't know why I bother inviting you for a particular time, it won't make any difference.' He then pointed out to me that he had made a deliberate decision about three years earlier to arrive on time and be generally more reliable. Thinking back, I realised for the first time that he had, in fact, been consistently on time for the last few years, and always phoned if he was delayed or couldn't make it. But I'd never noticed the improvement. Now, however, my opinion of his reliability has changed.

If you improve on aspects of your personal image, it may not be noticed right away. But if your boss comments when you ask for your rise that you often display a negative attitude, for example, you can point out that they'll be hard

pressed to quote a recent example of your negativity because you have been consciously adopting a more positive approach. And, of course, newcomers to the
organisation (including new managers more senior than you) will see only the
new, positive image and take it for granted.

no superman

Your mission is not to transform yourself, like Clark Kent, into someone unrecognisable (at the same time as working on the new skills
you've identified in the previous chapter). Simply make the decision to
work on those areas where you can improve your image and become
someone whom everyone sees as a high flier. (As always, you might
as well be honest or it won't work.)

personal appearance

One of the keys to improving your image is to be consistent. If you look smart
four days a week but always come in rumpled and over-casual on a Monday
morning, you are undoing the good work of every Tuesday-through-Friday at the
start of each week. If your company's dress code is informal, that's fine. But
make sure your clothes are clean and pressed every day – not just the days you
have important meetings. And dress appropriately for the job in terms of acces
sories, jewellery and so on, as well as clothes. Your hair, teeth and nails should
always be clean, and if smoking isn't part of the corporate culture, keep any evidence of it well concealed.

confidence

This is a huge component of success. You don't have to be big and brash – quiet
confidence can be equally impressive. But if you cast doubt on your own abilities, others will doubt you too. So if you're asked to give your first presentation

or meet an important customer, don't say 'Ooh, I don't know if I can handle it. I'm not very good at that sort of thing. I'm worried I'll let you down.' You don't have to pretend to be totally cool, but don't undermine others' confidence in you. Say something like, 'I've never done it before, but I'm sure I can. So long as I get plenty of support it'll be fine. And I'll enjoy the challenge.'

If you are – or feel you are – particularly shy or nervous, bear in mind that the better you know what you're doing the more confident you will be. If you are nervous meeting people, plan in advance what you will say. Practise in front of a mirror if you like. Decide whether you will proffer a hand to shake immediately or wait for them to do so first. Be ready and prepared and you'll have nothing to feel shy or nervous about.

The same goes for scary experiences like delivering reports, giving presentations, running meetings, and so on. Plan what you're going to do, go on courses or read up on the subject, and give yourself plenty of preparation time. With speeches, presentations and so on, rehearse over and over until you know exactly what you're doing. It does more for confidence than anything else.

energy

This is related to confidence, but it's not quite the same. You must have noticed how some people come across as being limp and mousy, or half-asleep, even though in some cases you know they are very productive workers. Others have a sense of energy and dynamism about them which is invigorating and inspiring to be around. They are the ones who appear successful, even if they're not especially so. When they really *are* good performers too, they are the ones who seem to win all the prizes.

Wouldn't it be nice to be one of them? Well, you can. We can't all have the charisma of a film star, but we can all inject more energy into our behaviour, and that's the key to appearing dynamic and capable of high achievement. Here are some simple techniques for boosting your image. You'll be doing some of them already – just add the rest to your repertoire, and get into the habit of projecting energy all the time instead of just on good days.

we can all inject more energy into our behaviour

- Speak clearly and don't mumble.

- When you meet people, smile and be ready with a firm handshake.

- Make eye contact regularly when you talk to people.

- Say hello promptly and with enthusiasm (again, practise all these in front of a mirror until they come naturally).

- Don't always wait for the other person to speak – be first to initiate a conversation at least half the time.

- Sound interested in what you say and in what others have to say to you.

- Move and speak at an upbeat (but not rushed) pace.

There. That wasn't difficult, was it? But it will make a big difference to your personal image.

positive attitude

If you're a natural optimist, you won't have a problem in this department. But if you're a pessimist (OK, OK, sorry, I meant a realist), you may find it tougher. The thing is, most people get depressed when they are exposed to negative comments. They find people who always look on the downside of every issue (as they see it) irritating and frustrating.

most people get depressed when they are exposed to negative comments

silver lining

Make it a rule that you won't ever bring a problem to someone unless you have a solution to offer, too. It may not be the best solution, but at least it gets you out of difficulty. So don't say to your boss, 'The new brochures for the trade show haven't turned up and the lorry's leaving to set up the stand in an hour. What do we do?' It's far better to say, 'The new brochures for the trade show haven't turned up, but I figured you might be able to take them when you come up on Friday morning? Or we could courier them – it's expensive but they're important so it would be worth it. What do you think?' Now doesn't that sound better? That's the kind of person your boss wants to work with.

Having said that, realists are important people to have around. They keep everyone else's feet on the ground, and ensure that potential problems are identified well in advance. If this is you, you're doing an important job; don't stop. It's just a matter of presentation. Carry on pointing out problems, but find a way of expressing them that sounds more acceptable to all those optimists you work with (sorry, woolly-headed idealists, I should have said).

There's a three-step process to making your realistic comments sound positive rather than negative to everyone else:

1   First, make all your negative comments specific, because that makes them useful. Instead of saying 'It'll never work' (a singularly unhelpful comment), say 'It'll never work because the costs are too high'.

popular people do better
at work

2   Next, never express a negative view without a positive one attached to it. So instead of saying 'It'll never work because the costs are too high', say 'It would certainly increase throughput, but it'll never work because the costs are too high'.

3   Finally, tone down your language so that you talk about 'worries' and 'concerns', for example, rather than insisting that things are 'wrong' or 'major problems'. So you might say, 'It would certainly increase throughput. My one concern is that it's going to be hard to get the costs low enough to make it work.'

You've made exactly the same point you always intended to, but now, all of a sudden, instead of coming across as negative you appear helpful and constructive. And you've made a valuable contribution by pointing out where the proposal still needs work. And all you changed was the way you presented your view.

likeableness

Popular people do better at work. They are more fun to have around, generate a positive atmosphere and improve morale. And as a manager being asked for a pay rise, wouldn't you be more sympathetic towards someone you liked? So if you're less popular than you could be, take a look through this list of likeable characteristics and see where there's room for improvement.

- Be a good listener.
- Show an interest in the people around you.
- Don't be arrogant or pompous.
- Don't gossip about people behind their backs.

- Never put people down.

- A strong sense of humour is a definite plus, but don't use it against the people you work with.

- If you manage your own team, be fair and always make time when your team members need to talk to you.

None of this is difficult, but most of us know deep down that we don't really listen properly, or that when we disagree with someone's idea we sometimes put them down ('That's a stupid idea!' rather than 'I disagree').

trust and reliability

You are bound to succeed better if you are regarded as being trustworthy and reliable. So make sure you never break confidences or act disloyally, for example by gossiping about colleagues to customers or suppliers. Equally, always show you can be trusted to get tasks done, especially when they are urgent or important. Show that even when delays have put you behind, you can still get the work done without mistakes. That means that when there's a sense of panic, your boss will decide to put you in charge of vital projects – you can be trusted to make sure it all runs smoothly. That'll give you a few feathers in your cap when you come to ask for your rise or promotion.

open up

People who are open and honest tend to be seen as more trustworthy than those who are private or secretive. It's not really fair most of the time, but that's the way it is. If you are a private person, try to be a little more forthcoming about yourself – you'll find it helps your image. You don't have to bare your soul; just join in talking about your holiday or discussing your favourite music, or tell the odd anecdote about when you were a child.

...ility

...rtant to improve your personal profile in the ways we've just looked at, ...f this may be of no use if you don't get yourself noticed. If any pay rise ...reward is going to be at the sole discretion of your immediate boss, this may not be an issue. But if decisions are taken, or have to be approved, further up the organisation, you need to be sure that you get noticed in the right quarters. When your boss breaks it to their boss that you're asking for a pay rise, you don't want the response to be, 'Who?'

All the techniques we've just covered – having energy, being likeable and confident and so on – will be a big help. But you want something more. You want your name, your face and your success to stand out from the crowd. Here are a few ideas that will help:

■ Make sure everyone knows you. Network within your company and forge as many links as possible with other departments – all ones that put you in a positive light, of course. So whenever accounts need someone to dig up some information for them, production want a trainer to run a course for them, or marketing need extra bodies to run an exhibition stand, make sure you volunteer. You'll meet other managers as well as your own, and become one of those people whom everyone knows.

■ Look for the high-profile tasks to volunteer for. If your boss is looking for someone to put together a report for senior management, make sure you offer to do it. If there's a presentation to the board coming up, offer to help. You may even be able to bring your experience to other departments – see if you can't get involved with an important project by offering to handle the press side of it, or put together a computer program for them, or whatever it is you're particularly skilled at.

■ Whenever you do come face to face with senior management, follow the guidelines earlier in this chapter to make sure you give a good impression and don't simply merge into the background. In particular, speak occasionally but not too often. At meetings or events we all tend to make about one really smart comment for every few ordinary ones (and the occasional really stupid thing we can't quite believe we said). We have one great idea for each half dozen mediocre ones. Well, when you're around top management, don't open your mouth until you've come up with the really smart idea. That way you'll earn an enviable reputation as someone who doesn't talk too much, but everything you do say is really worth listening to.

summary

It's not enough to be valuable. You have to be seen to be valuable. So make sure not only your boss but everyone else too is fully aware what an asset you are to the department and to the organisation. Make it an ongoing policy to have a positive and high profile all the time:

- Make sure your personal appearance is always smart.
- Be confident.
- Project plenty of energy.
- Look on the positive side of any problem or challenge.
- Be likeable.
- Be trustworthy and reliable.
- Work hard at making sure your good contributions get noticed by the people who matter.

4

chapter four

HOW TO WORK MORE EFFECTIVELY

Let's try a simple test. Here are some of the characteristics of two people; let's suppose they are colleagues of yours. All you have to do is decide which of these two people you think is the more productive worker.

Person A	Person B
■ Always arrives on time for meetings and appointments.	■ Is frequently late for meetings and appointments.
■ Always has the necessary papers, diary or whatever with them.	■ Often arrives without the necessary paperwork.
■ Always remembers to make phone calls when agreed.	■ Forgets to make promised call-backs.
■ Chases up suppliers, colleagues and so on when they forget to follow up arrangements.	■ Frequently complains of being let down by suppliers, colleagues and so on failing to fulfil arrangements and promises.

That wasn't difficult, was it? Clearly Person A is more productive, and Person A is more likely to get a pay rise than Person B for two reasons:

1   Because they work more effectively.

2   Because they *look as if* they work more effectively.

In other words, not only are their results going to be better than they otherwise would, but the boss is going to perceive them as an effective worker. Actually, Person A may not perform as well as Person B because they lack the ability, but they'll still look better. So if you're one of those people who claims that you work better surrounded by mess, I don't care. Even if it's true, it won't help you. Your boss will see you as disorganised whatever the truth is, and your chances of a pay rise, promotion or anything else will be damaged.

If you are already neurotically tidy and well organised, congratulations. You can skip on to the next chapter. But if you think there is any room for improvement in this area, read on. You need to improve your image as an effective person, as well as making your work style genuinely more streamlined.

Now, if you're not naturally organised, the idea of turning into a paragon of organisation is unthinkable. There are all sorts of reasons you can come up with against it. Let me guess:

- You're naturally unorganised and a leopard can't change its spots.
- It takes time to get organised and you haven't got that sort of time.
- Naturally organised people are all neurotic and uptight and you'd rather lose your job than turn into one of them.

No doubt you've got plenty more where those came from. Well, let's get something straight. No one is trying to turn you into something you're not. You can go on being a disorganised person, so long as you just adopt a few organised behaviours. What you do when your bosses aren't looking is up to you, but if you want this pay rise you'll have to make just a small effort to get into a few new habits. That's all. And once they have become habit, you won't even notice you're doing them. OK?

finding time

This is the *only* difficult bit, and anyone good enough to deserve a pay rise has got to be capable of managing it once they know how. Organised people don't manage their lives by instinct, you know. They have to have lists and notes to make it possible. The only difference between you and them is that they write things down that you wouldn't get round to writing down. That's it.

It's a small difference, but it has a huge impact. Because it makes them effective workers, so their productivity improves. Tasks get done in good time instead of being left to the last minute, and they have enough time for the crucial job of planning and working towards major objectives, instead of always running to

organised people don't manage their lives by instinct

keep still on routine tasks with no time for the big, important stuff like generating profitable and productive ideas.

pep talk

If you dread having to make yourself find extra time, just give yourself a good talking to. If you are capable enough to deserve this pay rise or promotion you're after, you're capable enough to find just a few minutes a day to organise your life. If you have ever managed to diet, give up smoking or keep a New Year resolution, you have what it takes to do this.

If you could simply find 10 to 20 minutes a day to do all that writing down, you could reap all those benefits too. There. That's the only tough bit – making yourself set aside those few minutes each day to do all the planning that will make you organised and effective. So when will you do it?

- You could arrive at work early and spend the time before everyone turns up – so long as you know you could avoid distractions.
- You could schedule time in your diary, so long as you don't allow it to be pushed aside for anything else.
- You could have a rule that you do it at the end of the day, and you don't allow yourself to leave the office until you've done it.
- Maybe you could find regular time each day on the train to or from work.

■ You could even do it at home in the evening, so long as it fits round the rest of your personal life.

The rules here should be obvious: choose your time but make sure you do it religiously, every day. Pick a regular time that works for you (regular so it becomes a habit) and *never* allow it to be edged out by other things. Once you start to fall behind, you're on a slippery slope. Inevitably this is the biggest danger for naturally disorganised people. But organise only these few minutes each day and everything else will fall into place. I promise. If you don't believe me, just try it for a fortnight. Once it has become a habit to spend this time, you'll find it becomes as easy as finding time for other habits such as taking a morning shower or eating lunch. What's more, this time is an investment. Once you're into the swing of the new system you'll find it generates far more time than it occupies.

organising your working life

Right. So that's sorted. You've cleared about a quarter of an hour a day to get organised, so what are you going to do with it? Before I answer that question I have a confession to make. I lied. Clearing this time isn't the only thing you have to do. But it is the only difficult thing – honest.

The other thing you have to do is really easy. You have to get yourself a notebook and a pen and never let them out of your sight. Organising is a two-part operation: you spend the day intelligence gathering, and then you sit down for your 15-minute stint to collate all the information you've assembled. During the day, write down everything that comes along that will have any impact at all in the future, whether that's tomorrow or next year. You should jot down the following:

■ Every time you promise to make a phone call later in the week ('I'll call you Friday afternoon').

■ Every time anyone says they'll contact you ('I'll get back to you when I've put together a quote').

■ Every meeting, appointment or event that gets mentioned that you need to know about – even if you don't actually have to be there ('We'll be discussing that point at next Tuesday's departmental meeting').

■ Every point for action that you think of or anyone mentions ('I must go and take a look at the new store once it's open').

Jot them down as scrappily as you like, in any kind of shorthand so long as you can read it back later. If someone gives you a memo, minutes of a meeting, a brochure, an e-mail, a Post-it note or anything else that contains information about dates, times or action points, keep them in a folder rather than bothering to copy them across to your notebook (which obviously just wouldn't get done).

See? This bit really isn't difficult. Each note you jot down takes only a moment, and within a couple of days you'll be so into the habit of it that you won't even notice you're doing it. And you should find that it gives you a wonderful sense of control. Everything you need is in that notebook – you're completely on top of the workload. There is just one vital rule: *never go anywhere without the notebook.* You must have all your information in one place (or all put instantly into the single folder you also keep for the purpose). If you start leaving notes dotted around the place, you're back in the land of disorder, and the process will stop being easy.

little and often

There is a simple rule to keeping organised: little and often. Whether it is a matter of keeping the diary up to date, tidying your desk, getting the filing done or working through phone calls, the trick is to catch up frequently so that the workload in question never gets out of hand. You'll hardly notice the time it takes to file two or three items a day, but if you leave it for as little as a fortnight you might have dozens of items in a pile you simply can't face tackling. Try to get into the habit of dealing with these kinds of tasks as they arise so you never get that sinking feeling.

the core of getting organised ...
is a well-planned diary

the diary

So now you're ready to sit down for 15 minutes at the beginning or end of each day. And you are going to transfer the variety of notes in your notebook across to your diary. All of them. For this, you need a decent-sized diary. Go and get one if necessary. You need one that has room for notes as well as having each day broken down by times.

The core of getting organised, working productively and looking effective is a well-planned diary. Boy, does that sound boring – the sort of thing a Monty Python-style accountant would have. But actually it's not so bad. In fact the feeling of control it gives you is rather enjoyable. And your 10 to 20 minutes a day is there to keep your diary (or should I say your bible?) in order.

As well as your 15 minutes each day, you will also need to find a few extra minutes at the start of each month for diary planning. In fact, you need to schedule four stages of planning, all very simple:

- yearly
- monthly
- weekly
- daily.

yearly planning

At the start of each year, you'll need to spend about half an hour (which you will have scheduled into your diary for the purpose) entering all the dates you already have details of for the rest of the year, such as:

- regular meetings
- special events (trade shows or product launches, for example)
- regular events (a monthly departmental lunch, or a weekly team meeting)
- holidays
- personal time (if you want to plan a day off for the kids' birthdays or leaving early on the evening of an anniversary).

You should also schedule:

- fifteen minutes at the start of each month for a similar diary session
- at least one full day a month – more if possible – for working on major proactive tasks such as developing ideas and planning productive new projects.

monthly planning

Repeat this on a smaller scale at the beginning of each month. Schedule time for things you didn't plan at the start of the year. This is especially important for managers, who need to schedule:

- selection interviews
- appraisals
- presentations (including preparation time)
- time to prepare reports and proposals
- time to delegate key tasks.

If your month is already looking overly full (and you know how many unplanned things tend to crop up so be realistic), now is the time to trim your workload if you need to. Cancel or excuse yourself from meetings you don't really need to hold or attend, delegate anything you can, and streamline your diary. For example, if you have two trips to the north-west planned this month, move them both to the same day.

two by two

Always look for opportunities to do two tasks at once if you can still give each the attention it needs. For example, do your filing (which you never allow to build up, of course) while you are holding for people on the phone. Or begin entering your notes into your diary while you're waiting for a meeting to get started, to save time later.

weekly planning

Once you're into the swing, this takes only five minutes on a Monday morning (or the previous Friday evening if you prefer). Start filling in some of the blank spaces in your diary by scheduling time for:

- delegation
- monitoring any staff who work for you
- catching up with phone calls
- dealing with miscellaneous tasks (these are the ones that really mess up your diary system if you haven't scheduled them – they push in and throw everything else out; Friday afternoons are a good time to block in an hour or two for this).
- taking phone calls – then get the receptionist or an assistant to field calls saying you'll definitely be available on Wednesday afternoon, for example, or before 10.30 on Friday.

daily planning

This is your 10- to 20-minute session that you are going to get into the habit of holding each day. Write down on the relevant page in your diary everything you have gleaned from your intelligence-gathering operations during the day:

- If you noted down that you would phone someone on Monday morning, enter it in the diary for Monday morning (with a brief note to remind you why you're calling).

- If you were handed a leaflet for an event you need to attend, which you stored in your folder, transfer the date to your diary (along with any contact phone number).

- If someone promised to call you back on Tuesday, make a note for Tuesday to prompt them. If they didn't give you a specific date by when they would contact you, write the reminder for whichever day you would expect them to have replied by.

- If you made an action point to write a letter, note it down for a time when you are scheduled to write letters, or to do miscellaneous tasks.

- Add into the diary any meetings, appointments or other dates and times you have collected during the day, and any contact names, phone numbers or directions for getting there that you might conceivably need.

By doing this, you will find that when you open your diary each morning, it will already include a list of phone calls to make and things to do, all entered over the last few days and weeks. If you find that you need time scheduled to work through these, simply make sure you give yourself a regular time. For example, you might arrive at 9.00 each morning but ensure you never make an appointment earlier than 9.30, so you have half an hour at the start of each day to keep on top of phone calls and daily action points.

prioritise

Organised people have all sorts of systems and codes for prioritising tasks. But the more organised your diary, the less you need to prioritise – it only arises when you don't have time for everything. But it is worth having some kind of code to indicate, as you make a note in your diary, if it is urgent that you do it the day it is entered for (just in case an emergency crops up and things slip ...). Pick whatever suits you – underline it, write it in red ink, run a highlighter pen over it. It's up to you.

summary

Having a well-organised diary means:

- Nothing gets forgotten.

- Action points – both yours and other people's – are regularly followed up so work doesn't need to fall behind.

- Tasks can be scheduled well ahead so there is no need to find yourself doing last-minute tasks (apart from genuinely unforeseeable ones). This is clearly more effective, and makes the whole atmosphere of work more relaxed.

- Everything is scheduled (or consciously abandoned if you can see there is no time for it), which means you never have to be late for anything. We are generally late because we've tried to slot in extra tasks, or find out too late that a task is taking longer than we thought.

- The important tasks such as project planning and planning to meet objectives are properly scheduled in so you actually have time to do them.

So keep a notebook with you all the time to make notes, along with a folder for storing memos, Post-its and the like. And spend about 15 minutes a day transferring these notes into your diary. You will need to have a brief diary session:

- yearly
- monthly
- weekly
- daily.

If you can find just a few minutes a day for this, you'll find that your working life is transformed. You will be organised, in control, on time ... in short, the kind of effective and productive worker whom everyone can see thoroughly deserves a pay rise.

There are plenty of other tips and techniques around for managing your time more effectively – and plenty of good books and courses on the subject – but getting on top of your diary, with all the concomitant benefits it brings, is the single most effective way to look organised and work more productively.

5

chapter five

HOW TO DEAL WITH PEOPLE

Your boss is going to be far more impressed by you if you are the kind of person who handles others well. If you are regarded as being pleasant and easy to get along with – but no pushover – you'll do well. You don't want a reputation for being difficult, petulant, domineering, submissive, negative or argumentative, or for having any other trait that gets in the way of everyone working effectively.

We've already looked at ways to improve your personal profile, and these will go a long way to building your reputation as someone who commands respect and is popular. But it helps to have a few techniques up your sleeve for handling tricky people, so that's what this chapter is here for. There are three techniques in particular which will help you earn the respect of everyone around you:

- keeping calm
- assertiveness
- feedback.

The first two of these are permanent behaviours which you can learn to incorporate into all your dealings with other people. The third is a particularly effective way of coping with conflict without causing worse problems than those you're addressing. One of the most useful things about all three techniques is that they are equally effective for maintaining good relations with colleagues, subordinates and people higher up in the organisation than you.

keeping calm

If you lose your temper, are easily upset, or frequently find yourself riled by other people – and it shows – you give the impression of being someone who isn't in full control of themselves. And if you can't control yourself (so the logic goes), how can you control a department/a project/a budget or whatever? If you want people to see you as capable and responsible, you have to start by showing that you are in charge of your own emotions.

emotional responses are never the best way to resolve tricky situations

Think about the people you work with. I suspect that the most highly respected people in your organisation very rarely fly off the handle, panic or burst into tears. Those people who do these things may be popular, they may be feared, they may be treated with caution. But they are rarely respected in the way that the cool-headed managers are. So you need to learn to stay calm under duress if you want to handle people in a way that will impress your boss.

When we respond emotionally to someone else who upsets or angers us, we generate a similar response in them. Suddenly you find the whole encounter becomes unpleasant, and the conflict can quickly run out of control. Apart from anything else, you make the only possible solution a win–lose one, which no one is going to want to lose. In other words, emotional responses are never the best way to resolve tricky situations – we'll look at better ways of doing this in a moment.

So resist any temptation to:

- get angry
- become sarcastic or snide
- burst into tears
- sulk
- panic.

Or display any other negative emotional behaviour, even if you feel it inside. Tell yourself that you are calm and cool, and you can handle the situation like an adult. And remember that every time you succeed, you are laying the next stone in building up your respect and standing in the organisation.

count to ten

Some people can be downright infuriating, and biting your tongue seems next to impossible. When this happens, get out. Make an excuse and leave the room until you have calmed down. You can simply say, 'I'm not happy about this. I'll talk to you about it later', and then go. If there is no way you can leave the room, just say nothing and count to ten under your breath. Remember that it is better not to speak at all if you are too emotional to speak calmly.

assertiveness

Most of us have experience of certain circumstances where we find it hard to express our views, to say no, or to stand our ground. We tend to give in for an easy life, agree to do favours we really don't have time for, allow people to walk over us or treat us disrespectfully. The trouble here is twofold:

■ It makes it harder to work effectively if you can't say no to demands on your time, for example, or find it tough to get your opinion across to a domineering boss even when it needs to be heard.

■ People will perceive you as being a pushover. They'll probably like you for it, but they won't respect you for it. And they won't see you as promotion material.

So if you've ever allowed yourself to be treated as less than an equal, or found yourself agreeing to things you don't want to do, you need a crash course in assertiveness. Here it is.

Being assertive is all about treating others as equals and calling on them to treat you as an equal too – on a personal level, regardless of company hierarchy. Assertive people neither dominate others nor allow themselves to be dominated. Becoming assertive takes time, as you start with the easy challenges and gradually build up confidence. But over a few weeks and months you can practise until you become confident and assertive, and begin to earn more respect in the organisation – as well as avoiding or handling previously difficult situations with ease.

There are three main components to assertive behaviour:

- Express how you feel.
- Be honest.
- Stand your ground.

If you can master all these, you won't find that you never encounter any conflict ever again, but you will find conflict less frequent and far easier to deal with. If you're naturally shy or low on confidence it seems like a tough challenge, but start with the bits that look easiest and, when you find they work, it will seem far easier to tackle the next step.

express how you feel

We've just looked at keeping calm, and an assertive person should do just that. But you can – and to be assertive you must – express your feelings verbally. Keep your emotional behaviour calm, but say how you feel: 'I feel upset when you don't give me a chance to contribute' or 'I feel angry when you imply that it was my fault the project failed'. It is a good idea to use this format ('I feel ... when you ...') because it is far less inflammatory than saying 'You make me feel angry/upset/put down'.

be honest

If you disagree with someone, say so. Of course you should still be polite, but this doesn't mean pretending to agree when you don't. You can say, 'I disagree' or 'I think your manner perhaps deters some customers'. Don't volunteer criticisms unless they are relevant to improving work effectiveness, but if asked for

if you disagree with someone,
say so

an opinion always be honest (but polite). For example, 'Your report was good, but I thought there were a couple of areas you could polish up'. If certain people don't really want honesty, they'll soon learn to stop asking your opinion.

stand your ground

Don't allow yourself to be bludgeoned – a popular technique among over-assertive people for getting you to do what they want. They keep asking until you finally give in. Well, don't stand for it. Just keep repeating your initial refusal – politely – like a stuck record. If a colleague asks you to come to a meeting to give them moral support when you simply don't have time, just say, 'I'm sorry, I can't come'. If they keep asking, just keep saying, 'I'm sorry. I wish I had the time but I don't.' Don't give in to intimidation, emotional blackmail or bludgeoning.

no, but ...

Most of us find it hard to say no, but you cannot meet your own priorities if you're always doing things for other people. So you owe it to yourself and your job to learn to say no politely but firmly, and stand your ground if necessary. But there is one thing which makes it a little easier to say no without feeling so guilty: offer an alternative. That way you're still showing willing to help. For example, 'I haven't time to do it, I'm afraid, but I can give you the relevant paperwork so you can do it yourself', or 'I haven't time, but Jo might have and she's good at that kind of thing'.

feedback

This is an invaluable technique for dealing with people problems in a non-confrontational way. If someone else's behaviour is causing you problems, this is the way to handle it. Maybe your boss persistently refuses to hand over schedules to you until the last minute, or perhaps a colleague is often sarcastic towards you in meetings. Feedback works with colleagues, superiors and subordinates and will resolve most problems without unpleasantness.

There are three ground-rules you need to follow when you use feedback to make sure you don't rile the other person into an emotional response:

- *Don't exaggerate.* Avoid phrases like 'You're late with everything'.
- *Don't judge.* This means resisting making remarks such as, 'Your time management is pathetic'.
- *Don't label.* Don't tell someone 'You're disorganised', 'You're a whinger' or 'You're a prima donna'.

You wouldn't like it if others did these things to you, so resist doing them yourself. Remember that the object of the exercise is to resolve the problem, not to score points.

So, bearing these three principles in mind, here's how to use feedback. Before you start, find an opportunity to speak to the other person in private when neither of you is hurried. Think through what you plan to say before you get there, and word the key phrases in your mind so that they don't include exaggerations, judgements or labels. OK, now you're ready:

1   When you talk, focus on yourself and not the other person, for example, 'I feel pressured and taken for granted when you hand over the schedules at the last minute.' As before, use the 'I feel ... when you ...' technique to prevent the other person becoming defensive.

2   Explain why this is: 'It's much more time-consuming for me getting everything to run smoothly when I can't set the ball rolling in good time. And I get a lot of stick from other people for being so late.'

you need to co-operate
to find a solution

3   Now it's their turn. Be quiet and listen attentively while they put their point of view.

4   They may ask you to give examples, so be prepared to quote specific instances to them.

5   Suggest a solution, and see how the other person feels. If you bludgeon them into something that they aren't happy with, it won't work. So you need to co-operate to find a solution. (If you can't see any solution, by the way, there's no point tackling the problem in the first place.) But offer something practical: 'I realise you're pressed for time too. What if I drew up a draft schedule for you a couple of weeks ahead, then you'd only have to check it through and approve it?'

6   Listen to their reply, and be prepared to compromise.

Feedback will resolve the majority of tricky people problems once you learn to use it. If you are a manager, teach it to your team and watch the levels of conflict reduce.

summary

Handling people confidently, effectively and coolly will earn you respect and a reputation for being calm and in control. And that's got to be good news when it comes to showing that you deserve better reward from your employers. Just master the three basic techniques:

- Keep calm.
- Be assertive.
- Use feedback.

chapter six

HOW TO
BE CREATIVE

Some people are full of ideas. Don't you just envy them? They have neat ideas for making things run more smoothly, and big ideas that generate income or positive publicity or better productivity for the organisation. They are known as 'ideas people', and they are the ones who get the pay rises and the promotions. Everyone can see how much they're worth.

So *you'd* better be an ideas person too, then, hadn't you? Why should those creative colleagues have all the ideas and get all the rewards? You know, there's a popular myth that some people are born creative and the rest of us simply don't have that particular spark. Well, cobblers to that. Believe it or not, creativity is a skill you can learn like any other. And you'd better believe it, because it's a skill you'll need if you want to keep earning pay rises and promotions.

The trick to having good ideas is simply to have lots of ideas. Creative geniuses such as Albert Einstein and the Nobel Prize-winning chemist Linus Pauling have testified to the fact that the proportion of good ideas doesn't change much. Pauling said 'The best way to get a good idea is to get lots of ideas.' If you have one good idea in every ten, you'll have ten in every hundred and so on. The skill of creativity lies simply in producing a high volume of ideas, and then sifting them to identify the winners among them.

change the record

So you need lots of ideas, and some of them are bound to be good ones. But how do you do that? Well, you need to find a new way of thinking. Obvious, really. If your current way of thinking isn't generating ideas, clearly a change is called for. The thing is, the way we habitually think is great for applying ideas, for working logically through projects, for dealing with routine tasks. It works, so we go on using it.

But there are other ways of thinking which, although less effective for these tasks, are better for generating creative ideas and solutions. They don't work well for routine use (which is why highly creative people, locked into creative mode, often function poorly in the real world; look at Van Gogh or Mozart), but they are just what you need for occasional use when you want to be creative.

creativity is a skill you can learn like any other

The trouble with the way we usually think is that it turns into a habit. Our minds are so used to following certain lines of thought that they no longer break away to adopt a more creative approach – unless we consciously tell them to. The skill of creativity entails learning how to think in a way that helps your mind to explore ideas and problems from new angles.

there has to be an answer

Much research has been done to indicate that one of the keys to finding a creative answer to a question is your own belief that there *is* an answer. If you set your creative mind a challenge, it is important that you believe it can be met. If you are confident that there is a solution, you are far more likely to reach it. As Henry Ford said, 'Whether you believe you can, or whether you believe you can't, you're absolutely right.'

Creativity is all about opening up new paths in your mind that you have previously not used. Don't allow your thinking to become stuck in a rut, but force it to adopt new methods. Set yourself a question – a problem to solve or new ideas to generate. For example:

- How can I spend my PR budget most effectively?
- What would resolve the bottleneck in production?
- How can Matt and I share a computer terminal without coming to blows?
- How can we boost productivity in this department?

Creativity is always linked to a particular challenge

■ What would ease the current conflict over the holiday rota?

■ What new products would most appeal to our customers?

Creativity is always linked to a particular challenge, so phrase your question clearly. That way, your creative mind will know precisely what you are asking of it.

the techniques

Now you're ready to be as creative a thinker as anyone else. You've decided what question to address your creative skills to, and you have simply to choose a new way of thinking about the question. There are dozens of techniques for creative thinking; here are a few of the quickest and most simple to use.

problem reversal

This is a quick and easy creativity technique. All you have to do is to phrase your problem – for example 'everyone wants to go on holiday at the same time' – and then reverse it. So you might get 'no one wants to go on holiday at all'. (If there's more than one way to reverse the phrase it doesn't matter, so long as you generate a phrase that describes a broadly opposite problem.) Now try to think of solutions to this reversed problem. How about these:

■ We close the business for a specified holiday so everyone goes on holiday at once.

■ We pay people to go on holiday.

■ We allocate holidays to people.

You might be wondering where this has got you. Well, it's opened up new channels of thinking, that's what. You can now look at these apparently barmy ideas and use them to generate new and feasible ideas to the real problem:

■ Closing down for a standard holiday period might lead you to think about whether it really matters if everyone wants their holiday at the same time. Maybe for the price of a temp or two the department could work around a couple of weeks with almost no one at work.

■ Paying people to go on holiday sounds pretty daft. But what about offering some people a bonus if they agree to forego some of their holiday, or to take it at an unpopular time? It would ease the pressures of understaffing.

■ Allocating holidays from on high isn't likely to go down well. But perhaps those people who want to take holidays on oversubscribed dates could work out their own system of allocation. It can't be hard to persuade them that a solution needs to be found – either they find it themselves or it may have to be imposed on them. They can draw lots, or maybe have a rota system – if you choose first this summer you get last choice at Christmas.

You see, this is a quick and simple technique for coming up with some original options. Everyone is different – you would probably have come up with different solutions from the same problem reversal. That's fine. So long as you generate original and realistic ideas, you can present creative solutions to your team – preferably a choice of creative solutions.

stay cool

Although these techniques are effective whatever your mood, you will find that the more you can relax the better you free up your unconscious mind to generate creative ideas for you. I know this isn't a great moment to say this with a crucial decision impending but ... try to relax.

see how thinking about sugar
can help to stimulate ideas

random stimulation

Like most creativity techniques, this one's fun too. And fast. The idea is really to knock your mind sideways into a different way of thinking – so you come up with different ideas from last time.

Start by selecting a word at random. Try opening a dictionary with your eyes shut, pointing at a word, and then opening your eyes. This is the word you have to work with. If you haven't got a dictionary to hand, pick the name of the first object you see, or take a random word from another book. Suppose you pick the word 'sugar'. Now think about sugar for a while:

- It's sweet.
- It comes from a plant.
- It comes in lumps or grains.
- You can eat it.
- There are lots of varieties.
- It makes you fat.

It's up to you what attributes of sugar you come up with. You don't have to be comprehensive. After thinking about it for a while, go back to your holiday rota problem and think about the two things in tandem – sugar and holiday rotas. See how thinking about sugar can help to stimulate ideas:

- Sugar makes you fat, so you need to exercise to lose weight. Maybe some of your employees might trade part of their holiday entitlement for member-ship of a good local gym. That would ease the pressure. Or maybe everyone would co-operate better if the company offered a free weekend at a health farm for the whole team in exchange for two days' fewer holiday each and an amicable settlement of dates.

- Sugar comes in lumps or grains – and holidays come in weeks or days. Perhaps people who take no more than four days' holiday at a time could be given an extra two days a year. Or those who avoid July and August could earn an extra entitlement.

- Thinking about sugar being sweet might make you think of sweeteners. How can you tempt people to give up their favourite holiday dates? Could you lay on some exciting event in the middle of the coveted holiday period to persuade people to stay? A meal at the best restaurant in town? A team weekend away?

Don't worry about whether you have the authority to implement these ideas. Once you've decided which are workable, you can present them to whoever does have the authority. If they are effective, you'll still get at least some of the credit – all if you're lucky. If the person you bring the idea to is the one who decides whether you get your rise, it doesn't matter if no one else knows it was your idea so long as they do.

drawing techniques

The creative function is located in the right side of the brain, along with visual perception, while verbal skills are handled in the left brain. So if you use visual rather than verbal techniques they can connect with your creative powers more readily since they are closer together. This is why many people find that doodling and drawing are more creative than verbal techniques.

One of the simplest methods is simply to draw the challenge as you see it. To deal with the oversubscribed holiday period problem, for example, you might decide to draw lots of aeroplanes all over the page, or a long line of suitcases. Maybe you would draw an empty office building, or a ridiculously crowded palm-fringed beach. We're all different, and the idea is simply to draw whatever comes into your head. You're exercising the creative side of your brain to doodle or draw, and you are focusing on the problem or challenge at the same time. The result is very often that you stimulate an idea that leads you to a new and creative solution.

Doodles are more abstract than drawings, and some people find this free-form approach more stimulating. The idea is to concentrate on your challenge while you just doodle at random. When you've filled the page, look at what you've drawn and you should see shapes or patterns that give you a new perspective on the question.

wacky doodles

If you find doodling effective and you want to vary the doodles you do to bring a more creative, unconscious energy to bear, try something like:

■ finger painting doodles or using an airbrush

■ doodling with your eyes closed

■ doodling with the hand you don't normally use.

keep out of the rut

You should find that these techniques are a big help when it comes to being more creative. However, if you keep using the same techniques over and over, your mind will simply create a new rut to get stuck in. It's essential to break with habitual patterns by varying the techniques you use.

There are plenty of books on business creativity; if you want to discover more techniques you can easily find them. You'll also find techniques for being creative in a group – especially valuable if you're a manager. If you can earn a reputation for leading a creative team, that will give you even more clout when it comes to getting those extra rewards.

summary

In order to be creative you need to train your mind to think in new, more creative patterns. Learn a few basic creativity techniques and apply them to any question or challenge that you feel calls for a creative solution. And remember that the more ideas you generate in total, the more good ideas there will be among them.

7

chapter seven

HOW TO GENERATE SUCCESS

What is your boss going to be looking for when you ask for your rise? Successes – positive achievements above and beyond what you're already being paid for – that's what. All the skills we've been looking at so far are valuable because they help to create successes. But without those successes at the end, they are worthless. You've got to be able to show that you:

■ resolved a production problem no one else could

■ brought in contracts that were particularly difficult to win

■ met and exceeded your targets

■ ran an event that not only went smoothly but got rave reviews in the trade press, or brought letters of congratulation from customers

■ brought complaint levels down lower than they have been for ten years

■ speeded up the order processing system so that customers now get their goods delivered 48 hours earlier than they used to

... and so on. These are the kind of achievements that make it singularly diffi-cult for your boss to refuse your request for a higher reward from the organisa-tion.

Every so often you have a lucky fluke – maybe a customer places a big order because they've taken a liking to you; your red hair reminds them of a favourite dog they owned as a child. And sometimes it gets better than fluke: maybe you have a flash of inspiration and produce a terrific idea. But real, solid, consistent success needs to be planned for and worked at. It's no good leaving it to chance. There are ways of making sure you generate a steady stream of successes, and all the skills we've covered so far will go towards doing just that.

make time for success

There's no way anyone can plan for success if they spend their whole time just running to keep still. It takes time to generate and execute successes, and you need to be able to find that time. The time management skills we've already looked at (pages 37–46) are the key to this – and this is one major reason why

it takes time to generate and execute successes

they are so important. Without the skill to schedule your time effectively you will be unable to pull off the kind of successes you need to justify a pay rise or promotion.

So when you have your yearly and monthly diary sessions you need to block in time for working pro-actively on creating successes. To do this you need sizeable blocks of time – half and whole days – not just the odd half hour here and there. Make sure you allocate yourself at least a day a month (or two half days), but allow more time if you can.

The big mistake most people make (who get this far) is eating away at this time to fit in other tasks or appointments when diary time gets tight. If you want to be a success, you have to recognise that this is the most important time in your diary and the very *last* thing to give when your schedule is under pressure. The physical page may look blank in the diary, but the time should be far from empty. Cancel meetings, give up lunch breaks, stay late to catch up, but *never* sacrifice your success planning days.

name the day

If you think you may be tempted to allocate this diary time to other things, make it harder by the way you mark the pages in your diary. If you scribble all over them you'll find it psychologically easier to avoid writing in other meetings or appointments than if they look empty. Or give them a name that reminds you that you don't want to eat away at them: write SUCCESS right across the page, or EARNING MY PAY RISE – anything to deter you from reallocating the time.

plan your achievements

So now you've set aside time for creating successes, what exactly are you going to do with it? You've got to decide what sort of successes you want to generate. And the most valuable ones are the ones that help you to achieve your core objective. And what is your core objective? You should know this – you should have been told when you started the job. But if not, you can work it out for yourself.

establish your objective

Ask yourself: what am I here for? Why – in broad terms – does the organisation employ me? Here are some possible answers, which depend on the department you work for:

- Sales: increase profits.
- Accounts: ensure accurate, helpful billing and/or payment systems.
- Production: improve productivity.
- PR: increase positive public awareness.
- Distribution: ensure fast, high-quality distribution at minimum cost.
- Marketing: attract new customers.

These are only examples – you may know that your objective is different. For example, you might work in marketing but know that your core objective is to build customer loyalty.

So decide what your objective is and then aim to create successes that further this objective. Your personal targets should have been set – by your boss in consultation with you – to help you achieve this objective. So anything you do that helps you to exceed your targets will be ideal in creating achievements that will earn you big brownie points.

threats and opportunities

You've established your objective now, but how can you use this information to notch up significant achievements? It's a good idea to start by identifying the biggest threats and opportunities your department faces. (This is the sort of clear, productive thinking you can do during those times you set aside in your diary.) Draw up a list of key threats and another of key opportunities. Let's suppose you work in the distribution department. Your lists might look like this:

Threats:

- Rising cost of packaging materials.
- Unreliability of ageing vehicle fleet.
- Poor flexibility makes it hard to customise service.

Opportunities:

- New despatch methods can mean faster delivery.
- Upgrade of delivery fleet could give opportunity to change system.
- Expansion of department into new and larger building.

The most significant threats and opportunities are the ones that impinge directly on your overall objective. If your objective is to attract new customers, the threat of increased competition (which could reduce your level of new customers) is more important than the threat of losing a key staff member – important though that is.

You need list only the two or three biggest threats and opportunities. Once you've successfully dealt with them you can return to this process and identify the next batch in a few weeks or months. What you are doing now is locating the most valuable areas to create successes at the moment.

When it comes to developing these successes you can choose which you tackle, and deal with as many as you comfortably can at one time. A big project might take up all your available time, while two or three smaller ones could run concurrently. If you tackle threats, you'll be looking for creative and effective ways to cope with problems so that the department can still meet its objective. Any opportunities you decide to tackle will demand creative ideas so the department can capitalise on the potential. Either way, and depending on the threat or opportunity in question, you will certainly need to find solutions and you may also have to carry them through yourself.

success begins at home

Successes that you can both plan and carry out yourself will earn you most brownie points, so pick ones that are within your own direct responsibility if you can. However, if you have no significant challenges facing you personally at work, but think you could solve a problem or generate achievements for the wider department, by all means go ahead and work on these.

generate ideas

Look at your lists and decide which threat or opportunity you're going to tackle first. Now you need to use some of that crucial time you've set aside in your diary to find ideas for turning the theory into practical success. There are various ways you can spend your time to achieve this:

■ Talk to colleagues.

■ Talk to your boss and to other managers.

■ Read newspaper and trade press articles.

■ Do relevant research on the internet.

■ Get prices from suppliers.

■ Use creativity techniques – alone or with colleagues – to generate ideas.

Which approach you use will depend on the nature of the challenge. Most probably you will need to combine several of them to create a rounded solution that is both feasible and has a high chance of success.

write down your ideas and submit them as a proposal

use the ideas

You may or may not be in a position to carry out your newly devised plan. If you are the manager, or have responsibility for the problem or challenge you are working on, you can go ahead (with any approvals you need) and get on with it. But maybe you are the bought ledger supervisor and can see a way to revolutionise the customer accounts system for the better. Or perhaps you're a sales manager and have found a solution for reducing complaints that hangs on a change in production.

If this is the case, don't simply talk to the relevant manager or your own boss – except as part of the process of generating a solution. It is far better to write down your ideas and submit them as a proposal. This may be as short as a single page, or it may be three or four pages. But put your name on it and present it smartly and clearly. There are two key reasons for doing it this way:

- People are less likely to forget that it was *your* idea that created the success. If they do, you can prove it (when you negotiate your pay rise) because your name is on the original proposal.

- Spoken ideas can get changed and modified. If your idea is mangled out of recognition and then fails, you can bet everyone *will* remember it was your idea – but they'll forget that the version that failed wasn't yours. Again, once it's in writing you can show that you had proposed all along that the new system shouldn't be launched without consulting relevant staff first, and that such consultation would have shown up potential glitches in time to remedy them.

None of this arises, of course, if you are in control of the whole operation from conception through to successful outcome. In this case you need to use the time set aside in your diary to plan the success you need, and to implement it. Even if it doesn't entail setting up and running a fresh project, it will at least require you to find time for phone calls, briefings, collating results and so on.

Once your ideas for success have been incorporated into your ongoing schedule – new systems are up and running, a new project is launched or whatever – keeping things running smoothly should be scheduled into your regular diary. The days (or half days) each month for working towards key objectives should once again become clear so that you can start planning your next success. That way you can keep 'em coming.

summary

In order to create successes you need to plan for them. So:

1   Make time in your diary for pro-active tasks such as success planning. And don't allow this time to be eaten away.

2   Establish your objective in your job – what is the organisation paying you for?

3   Identify the key threats and opportunities facing your department.

4   Come up with solutions to these challenges.

5   If you don't have control over carrying out these solutions, put them into a formal written proposal.

6   If you are responsible for seeing through your ideas, spend time planning and implementing them to make sure they are successful. Once the process is in place, start planning the next success.

part two

HOW TO GET WHAT YOU WANT

So you know what you want and you know you're worth it. But, as you also know, that doesn't mean you'll necessarily get it. You need to know how to turn theory into practice, how to turn a valid case for a rise into the real thing. If you simply walk into your boss's office and say 'I reckon I'm worth a pay rise' you just won't get the same results you will if you plan and prepare your case. How will you ask? When will you ask? How much will you ask for? What will you do if your boss says no?

All these questions need to be addressed before you go ahead and have the conversation with your boss. And behind them all is a basic principle: you have to understand your boss's viewpoint. How do they feel about giving you a pay rise or a promotion or whatever it is you want? In fact, how do they feel about pay rises in general?

Suppose you were in your boss's position (maybe you are – perhaps you also have your own team asking you for rises). You would have all sorts of things to consider before you said yes to a pay rise. For example:

- What will my own boss say if I start spending more on wages? How can I justify this rise to my own superiors?
- Have I got the budget for this? Where will I find the money?
- What if everyone else finds out? Will I be inundated with requests for pay rises and promotions? What will I do about it?

If you work in sales it is second nature to consider a customer's possible objections to buying from you, and be ready to counter them. Exactly the same thing applies to selling your boss the idea of a rise. What will their objections be? You need to be ready with arguments, facts and figures to persuade your boss that you deserve to be better rewarded, and that the benefits to them will far outweigh any disadvantages.

you have to understand
your boss's viewpoint

And you'll need to take into account your boss's personality. Are they a softie, or a hard-hearted bastard? Are they more likely to be convinced by logical reasoning or by emotional appeals? Do they have favourites and, if so, are you one of them? If you're after promotion, are they likely to feel threatened by you? Do they inherently recognise that some people are worth more than others, or do they figure you're already being paid to do the best job you can?

Your boss is a key factor in the equation. Unless you consider their point of view – whether or not you agree with it – you will be unable to judge properly how to go about getting your pay rise or promotion. In other words, it's no good simply being worth it: you must know how to persuade your *boss* that you are worth it *to them*.

This second part of the book is all about how you set up and handle the crucial conversation between you and your boss. It takes two to negotiate an agreement, and the more work you do on your boss's behalf preparing and presenting a case that answers their concerns, the easier it will be for them to say yes. You need to be on their side, not on the opposition. After all, you won't get your pay rise without them.

8

chapter eight

WHEN SHOULD YOU ASK?

The difference between asking for your pay rise at the right time or the wrong time can be the difference between whether or not you get it. So clearly it's essential to get your timing right. You need to judge the time correctly in terms of the business year and in terms of you and your boss's day-to-day schedule. If you want the best prospect of success you may need to wait a few months before asking.

the big picture

As far as forward planning is concerned, there are two key factors that should influence your timing:

- the annual salary review
- the company's performance.

salary review

By the time the annual (or six-monthly) salary review comes round, your boss has made all the decisions about who will get what. What's more, they'll have budgeted for these figures too. So if you come along and try to change it all after the event you're likely to get short shrift.

You have a far better chance of a rise if you approach your boss a few months before the salary review, when they are about to start thinking about salaries and budgets. That way, they can feed the results of your meeting into the system and they have time to adjust their overall picture according to the rise they agree with you.

Generally speaking, most bosses will be reluctant to launch into discussions about pay with you just after the annual salary review – they thought they'd put all that behind them for a few months. If your boss is likely to award you a pay rise between salary reviews, you might do well to wait at least a few weeks before asking. If, however, you work in an organisation where you have no chance of getting a rise that takes effect except at the statutory time – following the annual review – it doesn't hurt to start making noises now. A pay rise above the standard percentage is going to be a big deal in your organisation, so it doesn't hurt to lay the groundwork early.

So talk to your boss now. Explain that you would like to see a more substantial remuneration at the next review, and ask what you would need to achieve to warrant it. Your boss can hardly tell you that nothing you could do would deserve a pay rise – that would clearly be untrue and demoralising. That means they'll have to give you a clear objective: you'd need to double your sales, for instance, or increase your output by 25 per cent. Great! Now you have a firm objective, set by your boss. And when you meet it in time for the next salary review, your boss can hardly refuse you the pay rise.

get it in writing

If you get your boss to tell you what performance on your part would warrant a pay rise above the standard rate, make sure you put it in writing and give them a copy – minute the meeting at which you have the discussion, or e-mail them a summary of it. That way if they suddenly suffer selective memory loss next year when you tell them 'You said if I doubled my sales ...' you can prove they really did say it. Equally, if they leave the job, you can use this evidence as strong support for your case for a pay rise when dealing with their successor.

company performance

Your boss has to justify this pay rise to *their* boss. And it's tough trying to justify a rise if the company has just announced a drop in profits, or a competitor has brought out a new product that is taking market share from your company. Maybe new legislation threatens the business, or senior management has just announced redundancies. All these (in case you needed telling) are not good times to ask for a pay rise.

pick a time when profits are good and things are going well

So if you're planning to ask for a rise – or any other increase in remuneration – keep an eye on the company's performance and pick a time when profits are good and things are going well. Some companies grow steadily but you can still ride the crests of the waves. Others are struggling in the long term. If they are on the edge of collapse, I may as well tell you now that your chances of a rise are slim. But if they are hanging on in there, you should be able to win a modest rise, assuming you are well worth it, and so long as you pick the better times to ask for it.

choosing your moment

All of this should have helped you settle on the best month or couple of weeks in which to ask for your pay rise, promotion or whatever. Now the time has come to fix up a specific meeting with your boss. You might have been expecting to settle this whole thing over an informal chat or a drink together after work. But in fact you are far better off fixing up a formal meeting with the boss. The more professional format gives you several advantages:

■   It signals that you are serious about this – you're not just asking because it's 'worth a try'.

■   It gives you the opportunity to make a proper presentation to your boss, laying out all the arguments in your favour carefully. This can be quite difficult in a crowded pub, and in any case feels uncomfortable in an informal setting.

■   A formal meeting should mean closed doors, phones diverted and no interruptions – far more conducive to getting your boss to focus on the subject.

■ Your boss will set aside time for a formal meeting which they might not for an informal chat. This means they shouldn't be constantly looking at their watch and itching to get off to their next appointment.

■ A formal meeting gives you an excuse to jot down the key points made and copy it to your boss later (whereas it's hardly common practice to minute your lunchtime trip to the pub).

So how are you going to ask? You may feel that your boss will resist the suggestion of a pay rise and that you don't want to announce in advance that this is the reason you'd like to meet. You can perfectly well ask for a meeting in order to discuss your work and leave it at that. If they ask you for more detail, explain that you want to talk about your performance and perhaps mention that you want to review your overall compensation package. You certainly won't need to be more specific than that (if they press further you can simply use the assertiveness techniques on pages 50–52 and politely repeat yourself).

don't jump the gun

It's possible that your boss will agree to meet and will suggest a time in the next day or two – maybe their diary is full all next week and then they're off on a conference. If you haven't prepared your case fully yet, you're going to be in trouble. So don't ask for a meeting until you're ready for it.

setting a time

Given a choice, when should you ask to meet? Tomorrow morning? Next Friday afternoon? The thing to bear in mind is that your boss is far more likely to say yes when they are relaxed and feeling positive than when they are stressed and feeling negative. So you need to judge your boss's likely mood and pick your time accordingly. Here is a big clue to help you – a list of good and bad times to meet with your boss.

you need to judge your boss's likely mood

good times to meet

- When you've just had a big success (maybe you know this month's results are particularly good, and the boss will get the figures next Tuesday).

- When your boss has a relatively clear day.

- When the company's performance is going well – maybe you know that good quarterly results will be published on Monday, or a prestigious sale will be finalised.

- When your boss is likely to be in a good mood – good departmental results, may be understaffing pressure will have eased on the team, or perhaps their own difficult boss will just have left for a fortnight's holiday.

- Times of day, and days of the week, when your boss is usually in a good, relaxed mood. Maybe they keep Friday afternoons clear, or stay in the office over lunchtime and tend to be free of appointments.

bad times to meet

- When your own personal results are not at their best. Maybe this month's results were good but lower than usual for a perfectly valid reason, but it might still be better to wait for the next really impressive success.

- When the company has recently posted poor results, or has just lost a key account.

- Days when you know your boss is particularly busy, and can't give you more than a few minutes between appointments (and what if they overrun?). You want to schedule a clear half hour or so for this meeting.

- When your boss is likely to be in a bad mood: poor team results, department under pressure, mother just arrived for a long visit – that sort of thing.

■ Times and days of the week when your boss is usually in a stressed or bad-tempered mood, or in a rush. Maybe they hate Monday mornings, or are always in a hurry to get away on a Wednesday afternoon.

whoops ...

Suppose you fix up a meeting at the perfect time and then something unexpected happens which makes it look like a particularly bad time. Maybe your boss is suddenly under huge pressure as half the department goes off sick, or perhaps your case is weakened by industry news that the sector is in trouble and you need extra time to adjust your presentation to accommodate this. When this happens, ask your boss to reschedule the meeting. If they are under pressure they'll probably be grateful. If not, simply say you need a little more time to prepare for the meeting and could it be rescheduled for, say, next week.

how often can you ask?

Here's a tricky question. Some bosses are enlightened enough to recognise that you can ask every day so long as you can demonstrate that your value has increased substantially since yesterday. Others get shirty if you ask more than once every three or even five years. You're going to have to take your own boss's view into account on this – a combination of intelligent guesswork, observing what pay awards others get and even nonchalant questioning should establish the answer.

There's no reason why you shouldn't ask your boss directly, but if they realise why you're asking the likelihood is they'll put a longer time span on it than they would actually accept in reality. Once they've told you directly that they wouldn't want to give a pay rise more often than once every two years, you've made it much harder (although not impossible) to ask them for another rise in a year's time.

aim to ask for a rise
as often as you can

Once you've established your boss's view as closely as you can, aim to ask for a rise as often as you can, making sure you can really justify it each time. If you can only ask once every two or three years, I'd wait a few months until you've improved your value substantially and then ask for a really good rise – it's going to have to last you a while.

summary

Timing your meeting with your boss well is important – it may determine whether or not you get what you want. You need to look at two aspects of timing:

■ the big picture – especially the annual salary review, and company performance

■ the right moment – in terms of the day-to-day timing.

In both cases you want to pick a moment when the boss is in a relaxed and positive mood, the company is doing well, and so are you.

chapter nine

HOW MUCH WILL YOU ASK FOR?

Oooohh, here's a tricky one. Tricky but crucial. Wouldn't it be a shame to win just a tiny pay rise when you could have got far more if you'd only asked? Then again, wouldn't you feel dreadful if you looked plain greedy by asking, pointlessly, for double the most you could possibly get? Most people fret about how much they should ask for if they want to achieve the twin aim of looking reasonable and winning the best pay award they can. So let's consider how to do it.

You need to start by asking yourself a question: why do I want a pay rise? Other than the fact that most of us wouldn't say no to a bit of extra cash, most of us decide it's time for a rise for one of two reasons:

- We need more money for personal reasons (a mortgage, another baby on the way, fancy owning a Jaguar XJS).
- We believe we are underpaid for the job we do and therefore feel undervalued.

If the first of these is the case – you need more money – you can probably work out quite easily how much you need. You know what the mortgage will cost, or how much your petrol consumption will go up. This is a useful figure to identify because it gives you a bottom line for your negotiations. *However* – and this is a big however – your boss won't give two hoots about your mortgage, your child or your XJS. You're not being paid to maintain a particular lifestyle, you're being paid for the work you do.

Your boss will only give you a pay rise if you can show that you fulfil the second of the two reasons for asking: you are underpaid for the job you do. As we've seen in the first part of this book, you'll have to prove you are worth more than they're giving you. It helps, however, if you're aiming to support a more expensive lifestyle, to know how much extra worth you need to prove to cover the mortgage repayments. That gives you a target pay rise to aim for.

**you're not being paid to maintain
a particular lifestyle**

score a few successes

If you cannot justify the pay rise you're going to need to support your lifestyle, have a look at the chapter on how to generate success and notch up some good results before you ask for your rise.

so how much, then?

The answer to this burning question has two components:

1   Bringing your salary in line with benchmarks inside and outside the organisation.

2   Being rewarded on top of this if your value exceeds the standard expected.

benchmarking

You're going to have to do your research, if you haven't already, in accordance with the tips in Chapter 1. You need to establish:

■   the industry average salary for your job

■   the average salary in your organisation for the same (or comparable) posts.

If you are still doing the job you were taken on to do, you deserve to be paid at this level. If your organisation pays way above average, I'd avoid drawing attention to the rest of the industry if I were you, and benchmark yourself against your colleagues. If the rest of the industry pays better than your organisation, it's reasonable to ask for your salary to be brought in line with what you'd earn if you left your job and went to work for a competitor.

adding value

Benchmarking establishes whether anyone doing a competent job in your post deserves a higher salary than you're getting, and has a fairly clear objective result. You can find out easily whether, for example, the industry average is £1500 a year more than you get, or whether your colleagues earn £120 a month more than you do.

The other half of the equation involves working out how much extra you personally are worth. Many of your results at work are no more than you are paid for. If you're a sales person, for instance, you are expected to bring in a certain level of sales in return for the salary you already receive. To work out how much *more* you are worth, you're going to have to list all the extra benefits the organisation is getting from you over and above what they already pay you for (you'll need this list again later on). For example:

- income you have generated for the organisation – directly or indirectly – above the level expected
- savings you have instigated
- increase in productivity in the team or in the wider organisation thanks to you
- extra responsibilities you've taken on since your salary was last set
- extra hours you consistently work beyond what's in your contract and/or is the accepted norm
- extra expenses you've incurred *in the line of work* – such as mileage now you've agreed to take a detour on the way home each night to drop the crates back at the depot
- any increase in responsibility for others – perhaps it's always you who stands in for the boss when they are away at a conference or on holiday.

Many of these should carry a clear indication of what you can justify asking as a result. For example:

- Suppose you are a sales person (to start with an easy example) on the same salary as your fellow sales staff. The average income generated by each of the team is around £100,000. It's fair to assume that this is what you're being paid to generate. But suppose your sales amount to twice that? How much extra can you ask for? Well, if you're earning the organisation as much as two sales people would, why shouldn't you get paid as much as two? You might not get quite that much, but you are sufficiently justified in making your request for it to look fair rather than greedy. After all, if you leave, they'll probably have to pay two replacements to generate the same sales as you.

- Suppose you found a way to save the organisation £4000 a year. What percentage of this saving could you reasonably expect to receive as a reward? You might not get all you ask for, but 10 to 20 per cent isn't an unreasonable request.

- What if you've taken on extra responsibilities? Look at what they are and how much time you spend on them. If a higher-paid colleague left and you took over half their responsibilities, for example, you've got to be able to justify splitting the difference between your present salary and the salary the colleague was on.

These examples should help you work out a fair increase to ask for. I can't tell you how much of it you'll get – we'll look at how to get what you want later on – but the aim at the moment is to decide what to *ask* for. You don't want to ask for too little, and you don't want to look greedy by asking for more than you can justify. This process will help you decide how much you can reasonably get away with asking for.

By the way, if you list several areas where you've added value to yourself, you can perfectly well justify asking for a reward for all of them. If you've doubled the average sales income *and* filled in for your boss during holidays and other absences, you can reasonably ask for double your salary *plus* extra for the added responsibility.

start by asking for more than you're expecting

mixed bag

You may not want a pay rise alone or, with a skinflint boss, you may think you won't get as much as you deserve. Bear in mind the option of asking for a lower pay rise alongside other benefits – a one-off bonus, health club membership, extra holiday or whatever you want. So long as the whole lot adds up to no more than you're worth, you can mix and match as you please. We'll look at this in more detail later (see page 136).

leave room for manoeuvre

There's one more important point to make here. You're going to end up negotiating this salary increase, and negotiation (as we'll see later) is a game in which everyone pretends to settle for less than they wanted so the other person feels good. In fact, all sensible negotiators start by asking for *more* than they plan to get, so they can sportingly allow themselves to be beaten down. You'll be doing the same.

This means you have to start by asking for more than you're expecting, but the game requires you to justify your initial figure even though we all know you're not going to get it. So if you think you really ought to get £2000 a year more, ask for, say, £2400 (taking into account how tough a negotiator your boss is). If

£2000 is fair, £2400 may be a generous assessment of your worth but it certainly isn't greedy (your negotiations may even end up somewhere between the two). So always decide to ask for a little more than you actually aim to get.

summary

You can only ask for what you can justify in your performance at work, even though you may have personal reasons for wanting the extra money.

■ Begin by benchmarking your salary against the industry average and against the salaries of people doing comparable jobs in your organisation. See if you should be paid more on this basis.

■ Next, list the extra value you bring to the job above what you are already being paid for.

■ Then work out how much you can fairly ask to be rewarded for each of these.

■ Expect to be negotiated down and make allowance for this when deciding how much to ask for initially.

chapter ten

MAKING
YOUR CASE

Now you know what you're going to ask for, the next step is to put your case together into a coherent proposal. If you have any experience making proposals – either in writing or as a written presentation – you'll know the form. If you haven't, don't worry. You'll know everything you need to by the end of this chapter.

The aim is to assemble all the relevant facts and figures and put them together in a way that convinces your boss that you are quite right – you are being underpaid for the value you bring to the organisation. To do this you need to cover three aspects of the subject in order:

■ the current situation

■ the reasons why it is unrealistic

■ your proposed solution.

Exactly the same format applies if you are asking for a promotion, a bigger bonus or any other perks.

The formal meeting you've arranged with your boss will give you the opportunity to speak uninterrupted in the form of a mini-presentation. However, your boss is unlikely to want to listen to you rattling on, quoting chapter and verse, for half an hour. You need to assemble the key facts only to present face to face, so that your initial spiel lasts about three minutes – ample time to outline your case. The rest of the meeting is for negotiating on the basis of this proposal.

If you were preparing a written sales proposal, for example, you would put together all the detailed facts and figures, and the supporting data, in an appendix. You wouldn't include it in the body of the proposal. In the same way, you need to have any details your boss might query to hand, but you don't want to put them in your mini-presentation. It is enough to say, for example, 'The industry average salary for a legal assistant is such-and-such'. Your boss may nod in recognition of this figure, or they may say, 'Nonsense! Where did you pluck that figure from?' If they do the latter, you should be ready to back up your assertion by showing them the relevant article or quoting the organisation or website you got your data from. But don't thrust all these details at them unless they ask for

you want them to hear
the key figures

them. It wastes time and it muddies the water too. You want them to hear the key figures – what you're paid now and what you're worth. The more unnecessary data you give them, the more you dilute the crucial information.

nitpicking boss

You know whether your boss is likely to argue the toss over every figure or not. If they are the type to get defensive and picky, make sure your data comes from the most credible and authoritative sources possible, and have all the material to hand. If you feel it will look pushy to turn up at the meeting with a pile of statistics and trade association reports, put them all in an envelope file and bring them out only if your boss expressly asks to see the figures.

the current situation

You need to begin by agreeing with your boss what your current salary is and what you are expected to achieve. Both of these are essential. Suppose later on you say, 'I earn £750 less than distribution managers in our other depots.' What if your boss replies, 'Yes, but you get bigger bonuses to compensate for that, and very few of our distribution managers get a company car like you do.'

Likewise, you might say, 'I've taken on extra responsibilities since I moved into this job', only to have your boss reply, 'But those were always intended as your responsibilities; we just gave you six months to assimilate them into your job.'

So before you enter into negotiation, you need to be sure that you are both reading from the same menu. You do this by opening with a quick summary of your present salary and responsibilities. The more comprehensive your assessment, the less scope there is for your boss to take issue with you. You might be tempted to overlook the generous pension contributions and hope your boss doesn't notice, but if they do the whole basis of your argument is scuppered. Far better to count it in and make sure you're *still* worth more than your total salary package amounts to.

So your opening gambit might be something along these lines:

- 'My present salary amounts to £25,250 including benefits. You pay me that in exchange for managing the distribution department. That entails seeing that all deliveries are sent out on time and in good condition, managing two full-time and four part-time staff, and liaising with other departments to resolve any problems they have which involve distribution. I'm also responsible for handling returns and making sure replacements are sent out promptly.'

See? You only need a brief summary of the situation, but it is enough to ensure that you and your boss both have the same view of your salary and your basic job description.

the reason why the current situation is unrealistic

There's a problem with this current situation; that's the message you have to get across next. Either:

- the salary is insufficient for the job you've just described, or
- the job you've just described isn't the job you find yourself doing.

In some cases, of course, both of these may be true.

'I want what she's got!'

Your boss doesn't want to hear that you want a pay rise because Brenda gets more than you and it's not fair. Competitiveness with other employees can look petty and doesn't in itself justify a rise – maybe Brenda has more experience than you, or performs better. If you're comparing your salary with others make sure they really are comparable. Then express your argument for parity not as competitiveness but by saying you believe you contribute equal worth to the organisation, and therefore feel undervalued when you are rewarded less highly than others.

So you need to outline the difference between the current situation your boss has just concurred with, and the real situation. This part of your mini-presentation will go something like one of these examples:

- 'I've been doing some research, and it seems that the normal going rate for a distribution manager in our industry is closer to £28,000. I feel I'm being undervalued by the organisation since I'm earning nearly £3000 less than average despite doing what I believe is a very good job, as you yourself said at my last appraisal.'

- 'This seemed a very fair salary when I took over the job, but I find I'm handling other responsibilities too. In particular, I spend several hours a week negotiating with suppliers over who should pay for goods that are returned damaged. It's a tricky thing to handle without damaging supplier relationships, and I'm doing a good job of it.'

- 'In fact, it seems that my salary is £1500 below the average among distribution managers at our other depots. And on top of that, I've taken on the responsibility of two extra full-time staff since we set my salary a year ago.'

- 'I feel my value to the organisation exceeds what was expected of me when my salary was agreed. I've made several cost-cutting changes to the department since I took over the job, and when Joe left I reorganised so that we didn't have to replace him, which saved a whole full-time salary.'

You should be able to see how these brief statements in fact constitute very strong arguments in your favour. It would be hard to disagree in any of these cases that a pay rise is warranted. Keeping it brief by mentioning only the key points helps to strengthen the case, but of course you can note down other responsibilities you've also taken on, or cost savings you've instigated, to bring into the discussion later on.

Now add any promises for the future that will also add to your value, so your boss can see that by being given a rise you will continue to give value for money:

- 'The way things are going, it would make sense for me to take over the administration of dealing with damaged goods, as well as handling the negotiations.'

- 'It looks as if we're likely to be taking on at least one more full-timer and another part-timer in the next six months, and there'll be the move to the new premises to supervise.'

- 'I'm already looking at more ways we can economise on delivery costs, and I'm working on a proposal for saving £3000 on packaging over the next two years.'

your proposed solution

Now it's crunch time. You've laid the groundwork and it's time to tell your boss what level of pay rise you're looking for, and why you're worth it. You've already worked out the figure (after reading the previous chapter), so now you simply need to state what it is and why it represents good value to the organisation. For example:

- 'I believe £28,000 would be a more realistic salary for the job I'm now doing, and would recognise the fact that I carry a large responsibility for our supplier relationships.'

- 'An additional £1500 a year seems fair, and is only a fraction of the money I've saved the organisation in the last six months. If I carry on making savings (and I'm happy to outline to you the plans I already have), the rise will soon pay for itself.'

- 'You'll appreciate that it is demoralising to feel undervalued, and I feel a rise to bring my salary in line with the organisation's other despatch managers is a reasonable request.'

special case

Your boss will worry that if *you* get a rise, everyone else will want one too. So make it easy for them. Give them an excuse they can use for refusing the rest of them. Make yourself a special case. Point out that you have performed exceptionally, or have qualifications or experience that others on the team don't have. Your boss needs this help to justify your rise to their own boss, and to reassure *them* that you aren't the thin end of a long wedge.

put it in writing

You would expect to put any proposal in writing, and this is no exception. A simple one-page document is sufficient, and you need it for three reasons:

- It gives you an agenda to follow at the meeting, complete with prompt if you forget any key points.

- It sets out the most important information for your boss so they can see it clearly in black and white.

- It gives your boss a summary of all the key points as a reminder later, and to show to their own boss when they have to justify your proposed rise.

So what goes into your written proposal? Essentially, the points we have just

a simple one-page document
is sufficient

covered – current situation, reasons why it is unrealistic, proposed solution – together with a few more concrete facts and figures. Let's take a look at each section again:

- *Current situation*. Set out your basic salary, broken down into any component parts such as typical bonus, pension contribution, healthcare contribution, and so on. List the key responsibilities from your job description.

- *Reasons why it's unrealistic*. Now set out briefly any key findings you've made about comparable salaries inside or outside the organisation. And list all the main points you identified earlier that add value to your performance over and above what you are already paid for. This is the place to list your successes: the income you've generated, responsibilities you've taken on, savings you've instigated, and so on. Follow this with a sentence or two to outline each way you'll be adding more value to yourself over the next year or so: responsibilities you'll be taking on, qualifications you aim to get, projected income you expect to generate, ideas for savings or for generating income, and so on.

- *Proposed solution*. Now state briefly what salary you would like to see and why you deserve it, remembering to make yourself a special case so your pay rise can be justified without unleashing a flood of unrefusable requests.

Every important point you wish to make should be on this sheet of paper: a one-page proposal to persuade your boss – and *their* boss – that they will be getting both a well-motivated employee and a bargain if they agree to your entirely justified request. Once you have this proposal document ready, you are fully armed and prepared to go into your meeting with your boss.

cards up your sleeve

Don't give your boss a copy of your proposal in advance of the meeting, or they may use it to prepare a defence (if they're disinclined to give you a rise, and don't have the benefit of your persuasive verbal skills). Not only that, but they might also use it to set their own agenda for the meeting, which weakens your position. If you want to stay in control, you need to start off in control. Hand them their copy of the document at the start of the meeting.

summary

Put together a proposal that will convince your superiors that you are worth a pay rise. Set out the key points in the right order:

- the current situation
- the reasons why it is unrealistic
- your proposed solution.

Have all the facts and figures to back up your arguments to hand, but don't start quoting them unless you are asked to justify your assertions.

Now put these key points – slightly fleshed out – on to a single sheet of paper. This mini-proposal will act as an agenda and *aide-mémoire* for the meeting, and provides your boss with a written summary of all the most important facts, which they can show to their own boss when justifying your pay rise.

11

chapter eleven

HANDLING
THE MEETING

You're going to need a strong case (which you've already pre-pared) and good negotiating skills (which we'll cover in the next chapter) to get what you want from this meeting. But there's something else you need on top of this: psychology. The aim is to persuade your boss that they *want* to give you a pay rise, and the better you handle the human side of the meeting, so to speak, the more likely they are to feel co-operative.

None of the guidelines for handling the meeting are complex behavioural techniques. It's simply a matter of acting in a positive and pleasant way, and avoiding anything that will put your boss's back up. The result will be a strong, clear and well-presented case for a rise (or whatever else you want) which your boss will be keen to support. This enthusiasm on their part will be a big help when they go on to talk to their own manager to OK your rise.

You don't need a book to tell you that you'll have more success if you're pleas-ant than if you're belligerent, but it is helpful to have a list of dos and don'ts to maximise your chances of coming across as a deserving special case whom your boss would like to reward fully. So here it is.

things to do

By and large, your best approach is to be yourself. It's tough enough going into a negotiation over something as important as your salary or position, without feeling that you also have to remember a list of things you are or aren't supposed to be doing. So read through this list, and take note of any areas where you feel you are weak, but don't get hung up on getting it perfect. Be yourself and avoid getting things very wrong. But don't panic that a single poorly worded phrase is going to lose you a couple of thousand pounds a year, because it doesn't work like that.

know your boss

Different people approach issues in different ways. Some of us are logical, some are cynical, some are touchy-feely, some are intuitive and so on. Think about

persuade your boss that they *want* to give you a pay rise

which kind of approach your boss tends to adopt, and then help them by presenting your case in this way. Your written document should be clear-cut and factual – it has to do the trick for managers further up the organisation too – but the terms in which you couch your arguments at the salary review can be tailored to meet your boss's natural style. For example:

■ If your boss is the logical, rational type, and maybe also a stickler for keeping a tight control on the budget, you'll need to show plenty of figures that clearly demonstrate the monetary value you contribute to the organisation.

■ Cynical or wary bosses are going to want evidence to back up any figures you provide, especially those that benchmark your salary against outside organisations.

getting the measure of them

If you think about it, you can tell how your boss is likely to respond to a request for a rise by the way they respond to other requests. Think about their response to proposals, to ideas put to them in meetings, and to other requests such as for compassionate leave or new office furniture. And consider not only how they respond to you, but also how you've seen them respond to other people.

■ The boss who likes to make fast, intuitive decisions won't want to be bored with detail, so you'll need to make sure you bring out all the key points fast.

■ Some bosses respond well to emotional appeals. This doesn't mean emotional blackmail or self-pitying whining, of course. But explaining that you feel undervalued will cut a deal more ice with these bosses than with many others.

■ Underassertive bosses will need plenty of good, clear, strong arguments to give them the courage to argue your case to their own boss.

These are just a few examples to give you the picture. You should find the key to your own boss's style if you think about the kind of proposals they tend to accept or turn down, and the way in which they prefer information to be presented.

be positive

As we saw earlier in the chapter on improving your personal profile (pages 25–34), a positive attitude is far more attractive and encouraging for other people to deal with. It puts them in a good mood, and that's just what you want right now. So don't tell your boss you're fed up and miserable about your salary; find a positive way of expressing how you feel (without being positive about your current salary, of course).

The way to do this is to be positive about everything else, and to imply that your salary is the only blot on the otherwise beautiful landscape that is your working life. So tell your boss that you enjoy your job, that you find the challenge of it inspiring, that you like the people you work with, that you see a good future for yourself in the company, and so on. Your only gripe is that you don't feel your salary reflects your full value.

listen

Your boss is going to have a point of view to express, and perhaps examples of your performance to discuss, in the course of your salary review. If you don't listen properly, dismiss their opinions or interrupt before they've finished speaking, they will be riled and irritated – not a mood likely to incline them to up your salary. So you need to go into the meeting prepared to listen properly and show you are listening:

- Make eye contact.
- Relax, but lean slightly towards them.
- Show you're listening with sounds and phrases such as 'Mmm' and 'Yes, I see'.
- Repeat back key phrases to them so they can see you've understood: 'So you set the wages budget by the end of July each year.'

It is important to listen attentively to your boss, not only to avoid irritating them, but also so you can effectively counter any arguments they make against giving you the rise you want.

listen up

If the guidelines for listening all sound like a lot to remember without looking awkward and stilted, there is an easier way: just concentrate genuinely on what they are saying and the body language will look after itself.

things *not* to do

So those are the key positive behaviours that will help to win your boss over. But there are also certain negative behaviours that will actively deter your boss from giving you what you want. There are classic ploys or characteristics that far too many people use, to their own detriment, and the most common and damaging are outlined here.

don't whinge

Whingeing is negative and depressing to listen to. It also implies a criticism of the person you're whingeing to – if they haven't done anything about it they are responsible for all your ills. So don't come up with a long list of complaints

envy is not a reason to give someone a rise

about how dreadful your current remuneration is. And don't whinge when you compare your salary to other people's (in or out of the company), or you'll simply sound envious. Envy is not a reason to give someone a rise.

If you allow yourself to be labelled as a whinger, you instantly reduce your value to the organisation – and this is not the moment to be doing that. You also run the risk of coming across as a permanent whinger, and permanent whingers constantly complain about their salary (without necessarily adding value to themselves to justify a rise). It's not a label that will help you with this pay rise or the next.

The thing about whingers is that they go on about the past and the present – you can avoid sounding whingey (if you suspect that you may be at risk of it) by focusing on the future: the value you will be bringing to the organisation over the next months and years. It's much harder to whinge about the future.

don't make accusations

You're not going to endear yourself to your boss if you say, 'You promised at my last pay review …' or 'You said my salary would go up by more than it did …', and so on. This doesn't mean you can't draw their attention to past undertakings, but don't put your boss on the defensive. Point out politely that 'when we last discussed my salary, we decided it would be worth reviewing it again around now …' or 'I had understood that my salary would be increased by at least 6 per cent at the last review, and I was disappointed when the increase was only 4 per cent'.

If your boss is going to be swayed by a reminder of past promises, a polite memory-jog will be sufficient. If they are not prepared to fulfil their promise (and you don't have a written guarantee), making belligerent accusations will simply cause them to dig their heels in further, I'm afraid.

don't put your boss
on the defensive

Usually what happens is that your boss genuinely has a different recollection of what was agreed. Either one of you has misremembered the conversation, or there was a misunderstanding at the time. If you accuse your boss of reneging on a deal they really don't think they made (whatever the actual truth of it), you are only going to make them angry, which is counter-productive to the object of the exercise – getting your pay rise.

The real point is that what matters is to agree with your boss that you are worth more than you are being paid. If you can achieve that, you have established that you deserve a pay rise, no matter what was or wasn't said last time. So swallow your frustration when your boss has memory loss – real or imagined – and get on with the more relevant task of proving your worth.

get it down

If there seems to be a disagreement about what was promised in the past and you want to be sure the same problem doesn't arise again, note down the salient points of this review as minutes or as a memo and copy them to your boss. That way you'll both know for next time.

don't blackmail

Never say, overtly or implicitly, that you will look for another job if you don't get your pay rise. It is quite pointless, whatever the circumstances:

- If your boss doesn't believe you, your credibility will be undermined along with your claim for a rise.

- If your boss does believe you, they will resent the threat and this will put them off giving you what you want. They may be prepared to let you go.

- If you don't really mean it, your boss may call your bluff by saying, 'If that's the way you really feel, perhaps you would be better off looking for another company prepared to pay more than we will.' Now you're in trouble, and you've completely undermined your request for a rise.

The stark fact is that few of us are as irreplaceable as we'd like to think we are, and your boss may be far more likely to call your bluff than you anticipate.

'Ah but', you may be wondering, 'what if I really am intending to leave if I don't get what I want?' Well, even in that case, there's still nothing to gain by blackmail, and it can still backfire. The mere fact that you are negotiating over pay means that you would like to stay with the organisation, even if only on your terms. If blackmailing gets you what you're after, you still end up with a relationship with your boss that has been soured by what your boss will see as underhand tactics. This will do nothing for your future requests for pay rises, promotion or extra benefits or perks.

There is only one technique that really works in this situation, and it doesn't involve blackmail. You start by giving your request for a pay rise (or whatever it is you want) your best shot, and giving your boss and their managers every opportunity to reward you appropriately for your contribution to the organisation. If they refuse, you go out and get yourself another job – one that you fully intend to take. Then you hand in your resignation and explain to your boss, pleasantly but firmly, that their decision to offer you less than you feel you are worth has led you to find yourself a job with an organisation more prepared to recognise your value.

If there is any chance that your employers might be jolted into paying you more they will make a better offer at this point. Perhaps they didn't realise that you were such a hot prospect, or maybe they didn't realise how strongly you felt. Or, very likely, they thought they could get away with offering you a more modest pay rise. If they don't make you an offer, it is because they would rather let you go than pay you more, in which case you're better off in your new job. It should be obvious that it is extremely rash to use this technique if you're not serious about leaving unless you get your rise, since you may well end up doing just that.

don't blow it for next time

Remember that whether or not you get the rise you want, you still have to work with your boss. What's more, you want to lay the groundwork for getting a good pay rise or promotion next time round. So don't behave in a way that is likely to be detrimental to your working relationship or you'll undermine your own position.

summary

Quite apart from negotiating skilfully, you also need to adopt the right attitude when you discuss your salary with your boss. In particular:

Do

- Know your boss.
- Be positive.
- Listen.

Don't

- Whinge.
- Make accusations.
- Blackmail.

12

HOW TO
NEGOTIATE

the really important rules of negotiating are few and simple

OK, this is it. Crunch time. You're sitting in the salary review with your boss and you've just completed your opening mini-presentation. You've outlined the current situation, the reasons why it is unrealistic, and your proposed solution. Now you sit back and wait for your boss's response. And surprise, surprise … it isn't total capitulation to everything you're asking for.

This is when the negotiating begins, and if your boss is a skilled negotiator you could find them running rings round you. You're in danger of finding you've agreed to something you're not in the least happy with, and you can't quite remember how you came to say yes to it. This isn't actually smart on your boss's part – if they want a well-motivated and high-performing team, it's in their interests to pay you what you deserve – but few bosses are this enlightened.

But never fear. The really important rules of negotiating are few and simple, and you're just about to learn them. They will scupper any dirty tricks on your boss's part, and they will give you every chance of coming out of the negotiating game on top. What's more, as we'll see in a moment, you can massage the boss's ego at the same time, because the aim is for *both* of you to come out feeling like winners.

win/win negotiating

The real aim of a negotiation is for both parties to arrive at a mutually satisfactory solution: both pulling together, on the same side, to find an outcome that works for everyone. But somehow that's not what it feels like. It *feels* as though you're lined up on opposite sides of a battleground each doing your best to score points at the other's expense. In fact, only a mutually acceptable solution ever works. If your boss really isn't prepared to pay you what you're worth, they

only a mutually acceptable solution ever works

won't. And if you're really not prepared to accept their best offer, you'll take your labour elsewhere.

But although the results of negotiating depend on both sides working together as a team, the psychology of the process does have more to do with a battleground mentality. And bar running away (in other words, being sacked or handing in your notice), neither side is going to give up the fight until they have won.

watch that ego

The reason everyone wants to come out a winner is the simple matter of not losing face. Even if your boss can afford to give you a rise, they want to feel they've made you work for it. You haven't got something for nothing out of them – they've used the leverage of a pay rise to ratchet up your performance levels. The bigger your boss's ego, the more resounding they will want to feel their success has been. So take this into account when you negotiate.

That may sound like a recipe for a very long and fruitless argument, but it doesn't have to be. Your meeting can be amicable and successful, and be concluded in half an hour or so, on one condition: that you both emerge as the winner. Sounds daft? It may sound it, but it is actually very smart. On a traditional battlefield you could tell who had won by how many people on each side were dead, and by who was left wearing the crown. In the modern battleground of negotiations, however, things aren't so straightforward. In fact, the only way you can tell if you've won is if you *feel* like a winner.

And that works to your advantage. Your task is to make sure that your boss feels they have won. If they feel like a winner, they are one – by any reasonable definition. So how do you make them feel like a winner without giving yourself the sensation of having lost? The answer is that you make concessions, you let them beat you down. However, as you'll see, you won't be making concessions without getting back something in return (your pay rise, and possibly other concessions too). And the reason you can let them beat you down is because you start by asking for more than you expect to get.

As we saw earlier (Chapter 9), you need to begin by asking for a justifiable level of pay rise – but ask for the biggest rise you can defend. That way, you can afford to be beaten down. Suppose you really feel you deserve a 7 per cent rise. But you could put forward a valid case for a 10 per cent rise. So your approach is simple: you ask for 10 per cent, and you allow yourself to be beaten down to 7. You've got what you wanted all along, and your boss feels they have knocked you down 3 per cent – they feel like a winner too. And that's win/win negotiating.

know your bottom line

OK, that's your boss sorted out – they'll definitely end up feeling like a winner. But what about you? How far are you going to let your boss beat you down before you come out feeling like a loser? You have to go into this negotiation knowing what is the least you are prepared to settle for. Otherwise you may come out with nothing. It's no good saying, 'Can I have a pay rise please?' and then, when your boss declines, saying, 'Oh well, it was worth a try', and leaving.

It's up to you to decide what your bottom line is. Maybe your personal expenses have increased and you need to get a minimum pay rise to cover them. Or perhaps you simply feel that you don't want to work for an organisation that won't recognise your worth. Maybe you want a bare minimum of a 20 per cent rise, or perhaps you'd settle for an undertaking to give you a rise in six months if you reach an agreed performance target. Your bottom line may be well below the figure you're really aiming for, or it may be the same figure.

know your bottom line
and then stick to it

The important thing is to know your bottom line and then stick to it. And, of course, decide what you'll do if your boss refuses even that much (although if you're realistic, you've done your homework, you're worth more than you're paid and you negotiate competently, there's no reason for your boss to refuse it). If you're not ready to hold out for the bottom-line figure, there's little point in negotiating. If you don't hold firm you might as well just say 'How about it?' to your boss on the off-chance they up your salary without argument.

leverage? what leverage?

You might be thinking that you have nothing to negotiate with unless you're prepared to hand in your notice. If you're not, all your boss has to do is flatly refuse any rise, and that's that. Not so. You're here because you are worth more than you're being paid. That extra value is your leverage. We've seen that threats don't work, but you can always find other ways of phrasing the point you're making. For example: 'I feel I'm worth more than I'm earning because of all the extra hours I put in. If those extra hours weren't going to be rewarded, I would have to ask myself why I work them.' You're not threatening to work to rule, but your boss can see that you have bargaining counters too.

By the way, whatever you do, don't give away what your bottom line is. 'It's for you to know and them to find out', as they say. At least, let them think they've found out by beating you down to it. But if you're canny, they won't ever haggle you down that far. If your boss finds out what your bottom line is, they won't stop until they've ground you down to it. So don't let them find out until they reach it. At that point you can, if you wish, say 'That's my absolute bottom line'.

And don't, whatever you do, cry wolf. If you insist you've reached your bottom line and then subsequently agree to drop below it, your boss will quite reasonably disbelieve you when you finally claim – truthfully – that yet another figure really *is* your bottom line. And if they don't believe you, they'll keep trying to batter you down and the pair of you may never reach an agreement that works for you both.

negotiating techniques

So you're ready to go. You're going to make your boss feel like a winner, and you're going to make sure you end up a winner too, by fixing a bottom line in your mind and sticking to it. So now it's time to look at the specific techniques of negotiating – all those tricks that will ensure that you arrive at a win/win solution.

find all the variables

Suppose you want another £3000 a year – that's your bottom line – and your boss knows there's only £2000 maximum in the budget. It's pretty hard to see how you're going to find any common ground, even with the best will in the world. So what do you do? I can't really answer that, because you shouldn't really get into this position in the first place. The solution is to avoid this kind of stalemate altogether.

And the way you do that is by finding variables – other factors you can bring into the negotiation. For example:

- If your boss simply doesn't have the funds at the moment, you could suggest that if they can give you a written undertaking to increase your salary by an agreed amount in six months' time, you'll settle for a smaller increase in the interim.

- Maybe they will agree a standard rise of 2 per cent above inflation for the next three years, instead of giving it all to you now.

- Perhaps you could agree a rise in six months conditional on your meeting performance targets.

- How about making part of your salary performance-related?

All of these are good examples of the factors that can help to bring the two sides closer together in a negotiation. And what's more, we've hardly started. In the chapters on negotiating an overall package and on negotiating extra perks (pages 135–148), we'll see how you can bring other factors than salary into play too, from holiday entitlement to the size of your office.

The more variables you have, the more room for manoeuvre there is in the overall negotiation. So think through all the possible variables you could introduce, both when you're preparing for the negotiation and during the course of it. Never stop looking for variables until you've reached an agreement you're both happy with.

get all the cards on the table

If your boss is a tricky kind of negotiator, there's one ace they'll be holding up their sleeve. They may well have concessions they want from you before they will agree to a rise. They might want you to agree to delay the pay rise, or to take on extra responsibilities. And if they are an underhand dealer, they will wait until the last minute to spring this on you. In other words, they will wait until you've pretty well agreed on the value of the rise and, for example, that it won't take effect for another six months.

what if the boss keeps something back until afterwards?

It's one thing getting all the cards on the table while you're negotiating. But what if your boss raises an ostensibly new issue just *after* your pay rise is agreed? Your boss may deliberately wait until the whole pay rise is settled and then tell you, minutes or maybe days later, that they'd like you to take on new responsibilities. They're banking on the fact that you won't have the nerve to ask for another rise when you've only just agreed the last one. Well, tough on them. Don't fall for it. If they can save a whole topic for later, so can you. Respond positively and enthusiastically, and as though butter wouldn't melt in your mouth, in the same way you would if you *hadn't* just been awarded a pay rise. Say something like, 'That sounds like a terrific challenge; I'd enjoy it. I take it my salary would be adjusted to reflect the increased value I'd be bringing to the company?'

And then out of the blue: 'Oh, and I'd like you to take over dealing with Philippa's accounts while she's on maternity leave.' Now, it's not that you necessarily don't want to take over Philippa's accounts. It's just that if you do, that will increase your value even more, and with it the size of pay rise you deserve. But hang on, you'd almost finished negotiating, and your boss knows that you were about to accept a 3 per cent rise deferred for six months. It's much harder now for you to backtrack and insist that you won't take less than 4 per cent, and you want it from the date Philippa goes on leave. And your boss knows it.

The way to prevent this is very simple: ask your boss to put all their cards on the table, and do the same thing yourself. That way, you can balance all the issues against each other. All you have to do is to say, for example: 'I want to talk to you about my salary, and I'd also like to discuss my performance targets. Are there any other issues we need to discuss at the same time?' You've made it extremely difficult for your boss to keep back the fact that they want to talk to you about covering for Philippa while she's away. If they don't mention it, and then spring it on you later, you have the moral high ground and will find it much easier to insist that it be excluded from the discussion, or that you go back over the other points you've agreed and revise them in the light of the new information.

every time you lose something, you also gain something

never give free concessions

This is a simple but critical rule for negotiating. All it means is that if your boss asks you to lower the amount you're asking for, or concede that you will wait six months before it takes effect, you don't simply say yes; you trade the concession for a matching concession on their part:

- If they say, 'I can offer you a pay rise effective from next January', you don't simply say, 'OK, then.' You say, 'So long as the pay rise doesn't drop below 3 per cent.'

- When they say, 'You can't have a pay rise, but I can give you a commission bonus', you say, 'If we do it that way, the commission would need to be at least 5 per cent of gross.'

- When they say, 'The best I can do is 2 per cent', you say, 'I'd need an undertaking that you would raise that if I take on any significant new responsibilities.'

You've got the idea. This principle is crucial simply because it means that you end up with a better deal. Every time you lose something, you also gain something. Just make sure the concessions you gain roughly match the value of those you are giving.

tough cookie

When you don't give free concessions, your boss will soon learn that you are a tough negotiator. They'll think twice about asking concessions from you when they realise that every time they do, they have to give up something themselves. And in the long term, too, it's a good

thing if your boss knows you are no pushover when it comes to negotiating.

agree to all or nothing

The way you reach a final settlement in your negotiation is by moving all the
variables around until they balance. So, for example, if the salary is going up by
less than you wanted, you won't agree to defer it by much. Of course you could
defer it by more, but then you'd want a larger or smaller proportion of it to be
performance related. Or maybe you're happy to agree to a larger proportion
being performance linked, but only so long as the return on good performance
is higher. It's as though all these factors are on sliding scales, and you are sliding one up as another goes down, keeping them all in a balance that produces a
settlement you're happy with.

The one thing you mustn't do is to agree to any one variable before you agree
to the rest of them. It would mean one of your sliders was stuck fast, and you
couldn't adjust it to bring the whole thing into balance. This makes it far harder
to agree on a final deal, and you may have to give more ground than you wanted
on one of your other sliding scales to get a balance.

So you want to outlaw from the negotiation any comment such as: 'Right,
we've agreed to defer the pay rise for six months. Now let's talk about how big
the rise will be.' Don't agree any such thing, and if your boss tries to railroad you
with a comment like this just say, 'We haven't finalised the deferment yet; I'm
still considering it. But I'm happy to go on and discuss the rise itself.'

rounding off

Once it is clear that you have found a balance that you are both happy
with, that's the time to sum up (or your boss may do so), outlining all the
key points clearly: 'So we're agreed then. You'll give me a 4 per cent rise to
take effect from 1 May, and I'll take on Philippa's accounts during her six-month

leave which starts in May.' The simplest thing now is to ask your boss which one of the two of you should record the outcome of the meeting in writing, just so you can be sure that it gets put down in black and white, for future reference.

Don't be surprised if your boss doesn't give you a conclusive yes or no on the spot. Even if they negotiate the best deal they think they can get to keep you motivated and well rewarded – within their budget – they may still need to get their decision approved by senior management before they can go ahead. If you've given them the salient facts and presented your case well, you should have set them up nicely to argue your case on your behalf. If they tell you they have to refer the decision upwards, ask if you can supply any other information to help them.

There are also other responses you might get which aren't the 'yes' you want to hear. These range from 'It isn't in the budget' to 'No one else at your level earns that much'. You'll find the following chapter useful for handling these objections, whether they come at the beginning or the end of your negotiation.

summary

The way to negotiate is to make sure that both you and your boss come out of the meeting feeling that you've won. If you start by asking for a justifiable rise but one that is higher than you are happy to settle for, you can allow yourself to be beaten down. One of the components of this on your part is to know exactly what your bottom line is so you can be certain you don't agree to a deal that falls below it. The key techniques for achieving this kind of win/win outcome are:

- Find all the variables.
- Get all the cards on the table.
- Never give free concessions.
- Agree to all or nothing.

Armed with these few and simple techniques, you should have no trouble emerging from your pay review happier and better rewarded than you went in.

13

HANDLING OBJECTIONS

Terrific! Now you know all about how much to ask for, how to handle the meeting and how to negotiate the best possible deal. But hang on, what if your boss won't negotiate? Suppose they refuse to discuss a pay rise with you? There are objections that some unenlightened bosses raise to giving a salary increase – or to discussing one anywhere near the sort of range you're looking for. So what do you do when your boss turns you down flat?

Generally, your boss will give you a reason. If they don't volunteer one, ask them. You'll find that an outright refusal tends to stem from one of only a handful of reasons. So here they are, together with the correct response on your part to keep some kind of useful discussion open. Look through this list, and learn those responses so that you are ready for whatever your boss throws at you.

'it's not in the budget'

This is a standard response, and one that may or may not be true. In fact, good managers budget for pay rises in line with their team members' increasing value. But maybe your boss didn't. Maybe the company is tightening its belt at the moment and your boss couldn't be seen to award a substantial pay rise when profits are falling.

Since you timed this meeting to pre-empt the annual salary review, and we've already considered options for deferring a rise, presumably your boss is saying no for the foreseeable future. But don't fret – you can beat them with logic.

What if the rise didn't cost them anything? What if they even ended up making a net gain from it? They can hardly argue with that. So propose that they give you a performance-related bonus each year (or month or whatever suits you both). You get a payment equating to a percentage of the added value you bring to the job. If you don't generate any added value, you don't get the bonus. If you do, you get a share and they keep the rest. You're both quids in.

what are you worth?

If you do a job where you can easily calculate how much revenue you generate, or what savings you instigate, working out a bonus is very straightforward and you and your boss need only agree what percentage you should get. But as we saw earlier, you can set targets for any job that you and your boss both agree represent added value. Maybe you will increase your throughput, take on extra responsibilities, work extra hours, generate ideas that produce cost savings elsewhere in the organisation, and so on. Offer to draw up a set of measurable performance standards that enable you and your boss to agree when you have added value, and how much you've added. Then schedule another meeting to discuss and finalise these.

Make sure you get this agreement down in writing, as always. It should represent a permanent undertaking to increase your salary year on year, no matter what the organisation's circumstances, so long as you increase your value.

'I can only offer you a much smaller pay rise'

Your boss may well agree to a pay rise of sorts, but one that falls well short of your bottom line. If you agree to this you have sent out a message that you are a pushover when it comes to salary negotiations. What's more, you will have come away with less than you decided you were prepared to settle for. So find out why they can't offer you more. If they tell you it's not in the budget, suggest they make up the difference following the principle just outlined above (making part of your salary performance-based). Likewise if they give you any of the other objections listed in this chapter, follow the guidelines for that response.

If you really cannot get your boss to budge, and you don't want to go so far as to leave the company, there's no point turning down what little you have been

find out why they can't
offer you more

offered. So accept it, but make it clear that you do not regard it as full settlement of your claim. In other words, let your boss know that you will continue to seek a full pay rise; that way, they can't complain that you keep pestering for pay rises. You've only ever asked once – and you're still waiting for a final and satisfactory answer.

There's something else you can do, too. Ask your boss, 'What would it take for you to award me the pay rise I'm asking for?' They can't very well claim that nothing you could do, however valuable, could possibly warrant a rise. So they're going to have to commit themselves to some kind of concrete goal for you. They might say that you'd need to increase revenue by 50 per cent, or get extra qualifications, or improve your financial skills. Whatever their answer, you'll be making sure it goes down in writing. Now you know what you have to do; do it.

'nobody else earns that much'

This is a popular response with many bosses, and frankly an irrelevant one. You should be paid what you are worth, period. If others are paid less, then either they too are being undervalued, or they are worth less than you are. Neither of these seems like a good argument for under-rewarding you. But of course, it's your boss who needs persuading.

What you need to do is to read between the lines. What your boss really means is, 'But if I pay you that and the others find out, they'll all want pay rises. And I can't afford that.' So what your boss really needs is an *excuse* for paying you more than anyone else.

Your boss probably needs an excuse to give to their own managers too, to allay precisely the same worry. So do them a favour – give them the excuse they need.

We saw earlier how important it is to make yourself a special case, and this is why. Your mini-presentation should have included this, and all you need to do when your boss makes this objection is draw their attention to it. 'Ah, but no one else in this department has my experience with the GZ109', or 'No one else carries as much responsibility as I do. When you're away, which amounts to as much as 75 days a year, I look after the department on your behalf.'

pick the right benchmark

If your research showed that your employer pays salaries below the industry norm, point this out to focus your boss on the wider picture instead of the narrow perspective of your immediate colleagues. Say, 'I don't know how much my colleagues earn, but I know what legal secretaries like myself earn in comparable organisations. And my salary is about 12 per cent below average. Is there a reason why you pay less than most companies in the industry?' Obviously you can back up this assertion, and you'll have shaken your boss, who doesn't want to find they can't compete in the job market.

'you're costing us too much'

There's a very simple response to this ridiculous objection: 'I hope you don't view me as a cost. I feel I'm an asset to the organisation. My contribution has increased since my last pay rise, for the reasons I've outlined, and I'd like a rise in salary to reflect that increase. I believe I will still represent value for money.'

This objection can conceal a deeper concern on the part of your boss: your proposed salary rise will bring you dangerously close to their own salary level. This threatens their status. The way to get round this is to show them that if they give you this rise, it will bolster their own claim for a pay rise. The only thing is, you can't say this outright because they won't thank you for suggesting that they are so status conscious. So here's your response: 'I don't see that I'm that expensive.

your boss may well
not like the system

After all, plenty of more senior managers here earn more than I do. If I can be paid £35,000' (the figure you're asking, not your present salary) 'that must mean that the managers above me are on substantially more – they certainly should be.'

'you're already earning the maximum for your job'

Oh, dear. One of those old-fashioned organisations that hasn't noticed the benefits of paying people what they are worth. This can be tricky, especially in a large organisation which is likely to be very inflexible. But there is a simple solution.

In organisations like this, your boss may well not like the system. If you've presented a good case for a rise, they may genuinely want to reward you, but their hands are tied by the inflexible rope of bureaucracy. So with a little help, you may find them very responsive. And the solution is delightfully logical: if you can't earn any more in this job (because the system says so), why not promote you? Then you can move into a fresh salary bracket.

In some organisations this can be managed by creating a new job title, if it isn't possible to move you up to the standard next position. When a new job is created, a new salary scale will have to be set for it. You could keep much the same responsibilities but be promoted from sales representative to sales associate, or from chief packer to deputy despatch manager.

'I can't give you a pay rise now; wait a few months'

This may be a genuine plea that now isn't financially feasible but your boss really will give you a rise in a few months. You can easily test whether it is genuine by asking for a firm date. If they give you one, ask to negotiate the rise now (at least in outline) and put it in writing confirming the date from which it will take effect.

If your boss isn't willing to do this, the reason is doubtless that they are simply trying to put you off. So ask what the problem is with giving you the rise now. They will almost certainly respond with one of the objections we've already covered in this chapter such as 'It's not in the budget', 'Nobody else earns that much' or 'You're costing us too much'.

positive reasons for waiting

Your boss may have another genuine reason for asking you to wait a few months for your rise, so you need to find out if this is the case. Perhaps they want to wait until you've got the qualification you're studying for, or maybe they are planning to promote you when Daphne retires and they intend to give you a rise then to go with the new responsibilities. So always ask why they want to wait.

'my boss won't agree to it'

The only reason your boss's manager won't agree to a pay rise is that the arguments for it aren't convincing enough. If you've done your preparation well, you will have presented a case strong enough for most bosses to feel they can pass on, so this objection is unlikely to arise. But it's another of those responses that conceals a deeper worry on your boss's part.

Even if your boss feels their manager may say no, that isn't in itself a reason for them not to ask for your pay rise – after all it will placate you better than refusing to ask, so what have they got to lose? The answer is that they fear their own boss will think poorly of them for coming to them with an unjustified request that they should have rejected without referring it upwards. It will make them look as though they've all but given in to your outrageous demands.

The way to appease this fear is therefore to make your case so watertight, so convincing that your boss can be certain that *their* boss will at least consider it reasonable. That way, they won't look foolish for recommending the rise. So ask them why their boss won't agree to it, and they will no doubt tell you what they think are the weak spots in your case. If you then furnish your boss with persuasive answers to these doubts, they in turn will feel confident of using these answers when their boss raises the same doubts.

'I've talked to my manager and the answer's no'

Your boss may well not have given you an on-the-spot answer to your request for a pay rise (or whatever you want), but have taken on board all your arguments and then put the matter to their manager for a decision. They will then call you in for another meeting, at which they will give you the final answer. Often the answer will be yes, or yes with one or two final conditions or alterations to agree between the two of you.

But sometimes the response will be no, or it will be an offer well below your bottom line. In this case, your first priority will be to establish the reason for the refusal. Having established this, you can then follow the guidelines we've just covered for whichever objection your boss's manager has raised. Just because you are getting the response via your boss, rather than direct from the senior manager concerned, doesn't make you any less entitled to a good, clear answer with a plan of action for working towards a future pay rise. What you want to know is:

- why you have been turned down
- what you can do to put yourself in line for a future pay rise.

If your boss is not prepared – or not able – to answer these two questions, you will need to talk to the manager concerned to find out the answers. Explain to your boss that you feel strongly that you need clear answers to these questions, and that you would appreciate a meeting between the three of you so that their

don't try to exclude
your boss

manager can put you in the picture (don't try to exclude your boss; they won't appreciate it). It's not an unreasonable request and they should agree to it, especially if they themselves were persuaded that a pay rise was justified.

They may decline a meeting, but agree to ask the manager on your behalf. In this case emphasise that you would like clear targets to work towards in order to earn a pay rise. You don't want a message back that says 'You'd need to increase your sales by quite a lot', or 'you'd need more qualifications'. You want to know precisely what level of sales you'd need to reach, or what qualifications you should train for.

If you are underpaid for the contribution you make, a fair request for a pay rise should get you the reward you deserve. But in the end, if you have a genuinely good claim and your employers simply refuse to consider it, you may need to decide if they are the right employer for you (in which case see the final chapter, pages 175–182).

summary

Never take no for an answer. Whatever your boss's reasons for objecting to a pay rise, you can always make some progress. Sometimes even the most seemingly unarguable objections can be overcome, and often you can still come away with the deal you originally wanted. Look through this list of likely objections, and learn how to respond to each one to make sure you can still persuade your employer to pay you what you're worth.

14

HOW TO NEGOTIATE THE OVERALL PACKAGE

Your salary may be the only form of monetary reward you receive from your employers, but it's unlikely. There are plenty of ways your organisation can pay you that don't make their way into your bank balance each month or week in the same way that your pay cheque does. For example:

- bonus
- commission
- overtime
- profit sharing
- medical and other insurance
- pension contribution
- stock options
- childcare contribution
- relocation costs
- company car
- travel allowance
- accommodation expenses
- home computer
- mobile phone
- health club membership.

All of these represent a cost to your organisation, although not all of them arrive with you in the form of cash. Or, if they do, the money is tied up in some way such as a pension and can't be realised at your whim.

I talked earlier (page 118) about introducing as many variables as possible into your negotiation. Well, these are all good examples. It may be that you specifically want an extra £1300 a year, say, in hard cash to meet your mortgage repayments. On the other hand, you may feel strongly that your overall package should reflect your value, but not be so particular about whether you are rewarded in cash on the table. This is when these variables really come into play.

know your options

Before you enter negotiations about your pay, sit down and work out every cost you generate for your organisation – overtime, expenses, bonuses, pension contributions, company car and all the rest of them. And list any other variables that your organisation doesn't pay you but that they might well do. Maybe they aren't about to start a trend in paying for childcare, but you know they have given employees their own mobile phones before now, so why not you? This way you have a list of all the possible variables you can bargain with.

make it easy for your boss to say yes

You may well decide that at least some – and maybe even most – of the extra reward you want could just as well come in some other form than in your pay packet. This has a big advantage because your employers will often be more co-operative about these kind of rewards. They have several benefits, either to your boss or to the organisation:

- The total pay rise can be spread over more than one budget – some out of salary and some out of expenses, say, or out of communications (for phones and computers). That way it looks far less drastic.

- A single large rise can be converted into two or three much more modest-looking payments. A rise of £2000, for example, might look excessive, as might an increase in bonus of £2000. But a £1000 salary increase now looks more reasonable on paper, as will the extra £1000 bonus at Christmas. And you'll still be £2000 better off.

- It is very easy for your colleagues to compare their salary to yours (assuming they can find out what yours is). Your boss knows this, and is worried that any pay increase to you may start a trend. But it's going to be much

many benefits ... cost your employer less than they benefit you

harder for your colleagues to find out the details of a mixed package, and then harder to compare it to their own. To your boss, this makes these kinds of alternative compensation a better bet.

- Many benefits can actually cost your employer less than they benefit you. For example, if they invest in a home computer for you, they will probably be able to buy it at a discount, and then offset it against tax. The cost to them will be less than it would be to you. You, on the other hand, end up with a 'free' computer.

If you think your boss is unlikely to be able or willing to find the full amount of pay increase you want, it is well worth considering introducing as many of these variables as you can. And then you can play them off against each other. For example, you'll agree to a smaller salary increase if your expenses increase to allow you to travel first class on train journeys, or stay in smarter hotels. You'll agree to reduce your request for an increase in commission if the company will pay your childcare costs. The salary can stay where it is if overtime is paid at double time instead of time and a half. And so on.

plan your position

Before you go into a pay negotiation, it is important to think through the possible alternatives to a salary increase and decide what you will and won't agree to. After all, it might be your boss who brings these factors into play first. Just because they may all add up to the value of the rise you want doesn't necessarily mean that you will be happy with the result.

If your boss converts your entire pay rise into pension contributions, insurance and membership of a health club you wouldn't otherwise have joined, you won't have a penny more cash in your hand at the end of each month than you

decide in advance which benefits
you do and don't want

do now. Would you be happy with this? If not, don't agree to it. It is much harder to decide on the spot what you are prepared to say yes to if you haven't thought it through in advance, and it may only dawn on you once it's too late that the deal you've just struck isn't what you wanted at all.

be creative

It's entirely between you and your employers what benefits you get in your overall package. You can be as imaginative as you like in your suggestions, and your boss can say yes or no just as you can. So suggest what you like. Maybe you live two miles from the station and you'd like a taxi to get you there each morning so you can leave the car with your partner. Or perhaps you want a budget for taking clients out to decent lunches. Maybe you don't need a childcare allowance but you want a dogsitter's allowance. Perhaps health club membership is anathema to you, but you'd value membership of the golf club. Commission may not be hugely worthwhile for you, but perhaps stock options are starting to look like a good deal. There are no rules – so long as it suits both you and your employer, anything goes.

Some benefits, of course, will save you money, which will increase the total value of your pay packet immediately (but remember to calculate in any tax liabilities that may apply). A computer, for example, *if* you would have bought one for yourself anyway, will save you money. A mobile phone (fully paid for including calls) will make you a saving on your phone bill, again enabling your pay packet to go further. And a childcare allowance will also give you direct savings.

So decide in advance which benefits you do and don't want, and of how much value they are to you. Maybe you're happy with 'invisible' benefits such as pensions and insurance, but you'd need them to amount to more in real terms to make them worthwhile. Or perhaps you need a balance – which you must establish in your own mind – between invisible benefits and those that you can feel in your pocket.

summary

It is often easier for your boss to say yes to rewarding you in some other form than that of a pay rise. Consider whether you would be happy to replace some of your intended pay rise with another form of benefit (or more than one). You can then bring these factors into your negotiations as variables – you can adjust each of them up and down until the whole package is in a satisfactory balance.

Decide in advance which benefits you will and won't agree to, and at what level. In particular, decide what level of pay rise you want to see that gives you a direct cash benefit or saving, as opposed to a long-term investment or a non-cash benefit such as health club membership.

chapter fifteen

HOW TO NEGOTIATE EXTRA PERKS

Suppose you want a bigger office? Or maybe you don't want an office at all – you'd like to start working from home. Or perhaps you'd like an extra half dozen personal leave days a year (in case the children have to stay home sick, or you have to wait in for the new dishwasher to be delivered). Maybe you want a better-sounding job title. Or how about a car-parking space closer to the main doors?

None of these perks is likely to be a part of pay negotiations because they don't directly cost the organisation (although some of them do indirectly). If your organisation increases your holiday entitlement but you still meet the same targets for the same remuneration, you've cost them nothing. Even refurbishing your office isn't a cost related directly to you: if you leave the organisation, they still have the office.

This means that asking for extra perks isn't the same thing as asking for a pay rise, nor do you need to incorporate them into the overall pay package. What's more, it's better not to as a general rule. If your boss says yes to a personal leave entitlement during a salary review, they are likely to set it against a reduction in overall salary increase. So don't give them the chance. Set the pay rise independently and then – after a polite pause – ask separately for extra non-financial perks.

How long constitutes a polite pause? Ah, well, that depends on your boss. And it also depends on how strong your claim for the extra perk is – as we shall see. But you shouldn't need to wait more than a few months at the most, and possibly a lot less.

perks vs pay rise

Although you shouldn't bring perks into a pay review (for your own sake), if your boss offers you a lot less than you are asking because finances are tight, you may want to fall back on asking for perks. If your boss genuinely agrees you deserve a rise but simply can't stretch to it at the moment, it doesn't take a lot to persuade them that you would feel partially compensated, at least in the short term, if they

ask separately for extra non-financial perks

could reward you non-financially. A tight budget shouldn't prevent them increasing your holiday entitlement, giving you an office with a window, or letting you work flexi-time.

justifying your perks

As we've already seen, the key to success when asking for a pay rise is to demonstrate that you deserve it – that you are insufficiently paid for the value you contribute. When it comes to non-financial perks you likewise need to demonstrate that you deserve them. But financial arguments – those relating to your value – aren't generally the most effective, since they don't equate directly with these perks.

You need to come up with a convincing reason why this perk would benefit your boss or your employer in some way. If your boss sees a benefit to themselves, rather than only to you, they are very likely to say yes to your request (assuming they can). So the trick to getting extra perks is to present them not as perks but as genuine needs. Here are a few examples:

- *Flexi-time*. You work far better early in the morning. If you came in at eight o'clock (and left at four) your productivity would increase (if you use this argument, you'd better make sure it's true).

- *Bigger/refurbished office*. You often meet clients at work and your credibility would be enhanced by a smarter office. The clients would feel they were doing business with someone with authority. A shabby office is slightly insulting to the clients.

with a little thought, you can make out a convincing case for most perks

- *Working from home.* Your productivity would go up. And your employer would save on overheads, and free up a desk in the office.

- *More trips away from the office (e.g. to trade shows).* You would learn more about how other parts of the organisation work, and get to meet more customers – the driving force behind any business. The experience would make you more valuable to the organisation.

- *Private office instead of open plan.* You would work far more effectively without interruptions. And you often have confidential calls to make to senior management which you don't want staff to overhear.

know the boss

The better you know your boss, the better chance you have of persuading them of your case. What sort of things attract their approval or sympathy? If they have a loathing of being interrupted and disturbed, they are likely to sympathise with this reason for your request for a private office. If they are naturally secretive, point out that you often have to make confidential phone calls. If your boss is a pro-breastfeeding mother, point out that you need privacy to express milk for your baby during the day.

With a little thought, you can make out a convincing case for most perks. And often they are a fair part of the truth. Sure, we'd all like a bigger office just for fun or to make us feel important, but you probably do genuinely feel embarrassed about inviting important customers into your shabby room. There's no chance that your boss is going to think that you'd hate to change offices but you're a martyr to the job and, well, if a bigger office is the only way you can do your job properly, you'll just have to put up with it. They know this is a perk for you. But so long as you can persuade them that it also benefits them, why would they say no?

If your request for a perk can be justified, you can ask for it at any time, without having to wait for a long break since your last pay review. After all, it's nothing to do with your salary, and it's going to benefit the organisation. So you're doing your boss a favour by asking, aren't you?

make yourself a special case

OK, there's one reason why they would say no. It's the old 'If I say yes to you, they'll all want one' routine. Just as with pay rises, your boss is extremely nervous of a stream of staff through the door all demanding equity with you. So, just as with the pay rise, you're going to have to provide them with an excuse for saying no to everyone else.

Of course, in some cases they may not need an excuse. Perhaps no one else wants to work flexi-time, or maybe most of your colleagues already work from home two days a week. Perhaps there are enough big offices to go round, or maybe your job simply isn't comparable with many others, so there's little chance of anyone else arguing that they have an equal claim.

But there are still going to be times when your boss hears you ask for your office to be refurbished, and gets an instant image in their mind of decorators swarming over the whole floor, and dozens of staff poring over upholstery swatches. So you'd better have a very good reason for refurbishing your office and yours alone.

Perhaps you are the only one who regularly brings clients to the office. Or maybe your office got missed out last time the building was redecorated. Or perhaps your office needs the most brightening up as it's the only one without a window. Maybe it's smaller than eveyone else's. Or, if it's a large office, maybe you could suggest that it doubles as a communal meeting room for the two days a week you're always out of the office so everyone benefits from the improved look. It's really not hard to come up with a reason for being a special case; it's simply a matter of giving it some sensible thought.

don't beg

There's no need to be coy or embarrassed about asking for a perk you can justify. Either you are doing your boss a favour – if the perk will benefit the organisation in some way – or you are making a thoroughly justified request for special treatment that you need and deserve. So it's not a submissive, 'Excuse me, sorry to trouble you but do you think, possibly, please ...' It's a case of, 'I feel this is justified and we'd all benefit, so how about it?'

what if you're the only one who benefits?

All of this is all very well, but how are you going to come up with a valid reason why your boss will benefit from, say, giving you a better car-parking space? Some perks are clearly going to benefit you alone, but that doesn't mean you've no right to them. Of course, sometimes the perk may not benefit the company, but you're genuinely a special case. If you can demonstrate that you have a particular need for a perk, you may not need to show any benefit to your employer.

Take the parking space. Suppose you regularly give presentations – more often than anyone else – and two or three days a week you have to load and unload your car with OHPs and powerpoint equipment. This seems like a reasonable justification for having a dedicated parking space close to the entrance.

But what if you do no such thing, and you just don't like having to walk 200 yards from your car to the entrance – whatever the weather – and back again each evening? We're talking a straight perk here: no benefit to the company, no special case. Just a good old-fashioned perk. How are you going to justify that?

you *can* trade off perks against added value

perks instead of pay

The answer to this one is that you *can* trade off perks against added value. It's really not worth asking for your parking space during the salary review and taking it in lieu of part of the pay rise. There's no need to do that. So long as you increase your value to the organisation constantly, as we saw in the first part of this book, you can ask for perks separately from your pay rise.

Suppose you asked for a pay rise three months ago and, since then, you've increased in value again? You know your boss isn't going to agree to another pay rise so soon – they're not that enlightened – but you can easily demonstrate that you are worth even more now than you were when the last rise was agreed. You've exceeded your targets and you've taken on yet more responsibilities than were planned back then.

So here's what you do. Fix a meeting with your boss and go through a similar mini-presentation to last time. Agree the current situation, the reasons why it is already unrealistic again, and your proposed solution. But this time, your proposed solution is different. Tell your boss: 'I feel another pay rise is more than justified here. However, I'm aware that it may be difficult for you to award a second pay rise so soon when you hadn't budgeted for it. So I'd be prepared to compromise by finding rewards that don't make demands on the budget at the moment. And if my value continues to increase at this rate – as I plan that it will – you'll be able to build appropriate pay rises into the budget for next year instead.'

Now you're cooking with gas. You knew damn well you weren't going to get another pay rise (even though you really should). But instead of putting pressure on your boss, you're letting them off lightly. All they have to do is give you a decent parking space and half a dozen extra leave days a year, for example, and you'll leave them alone. (Until next year, when you've already forewarned them to expect a request for another well-earned pay rise.)

summary

You can ask your boss for non-financial benefits separately from asking for a pay rise. This means you won't be expected to trade them off against part of your salary increase. You can ask for perks any time if:

■ you can justify them as having a benefit to the organisation

■ you can justify them on the grounds that you have a special need.

Either way, your chances of success will be higher if you make yourself out to be a special case for any perk that your boss may worry about having to give to everyone else too.

If you want a perk that you can't justify on these grounds, wait until your value has increased since the last pay rise. If you know your boss won't give you another rise so soon, offer to accept perks instead.

16

HOW TO
GET PROMOTED

Promotion works a little differently from a pay rise. Both are just rewards for an increase in your value to the organisation, but promotion relies on a post being available for you to move up into. There are times when you can create a new, more senior job for yourself, and you'll find a chapter on this later on (see page 167). But straight promotion usually requires more advance planning than a pay rise does.

Of course, when there is an opportunity for promotion you can double this up with your request for a pay rise. A promotion should carry an increase in salary with it, and this should be negotiable. But you've got to get the job first, and that's what this chapter is about.

can you do the job?

You must inevitably have a fairly clear idea of what your promotion opportunities are. Maybe there's only one person whose job you could move up into (if they moved on), or perhaps there are two or three more senior posts in your department that you feel you could handle. Whichever is the case, you need to assess your ability to do any job you would like to be promoted into.

So watch the person doing the job at present, and see how much of what they do you could take over easily. Remember to consider not only quantifiable skills but also less tangible ones, for example:

- Do they often have to take tricky decisions? If so, how do they take them? Do they rely on experience you wouldn't have, or could you make the right decisions as often as (or more often than) they do?

- Do they need to be good at handling staff? What qualities does this call on: assertiveness? Diplomacy? Tough negotiating?

- Do they spend time with customers? Would you be able to handle complaints as well as they do? What about making customers feel special? Or knowing when and how to bend the rules to keep customers satisfied?

You need to consider these skills on top of the more obvious ones such as operating specific computer programs or writing reports. If the person whose job you feel

watch the person doing
the job at present

you'd like is not actually particularly good at their job, obviously the question is: can you do all these things substantially better than they do? If they are very good at their job, however, you can compare your own abilities with theirs directly.

helping hand

Often the job you would be most likely to get is occupied by a colleague and friend of yours. Such people will often actively help polish you up to step into their shoes – so long as you wait until they are ready to move on or up themselves. You'll know when they're thinking of leaving, or angling for promotion. In this case get all the help you can from them to learn the skills you will need to get their job when it falls vacant.

Now you need to be brutally honest with yourself about any shortcomings you may have identified. Maybe the person doing the job at the moment is great at motivating people – you can see it's an important part of the job, and it's not something you're particularly cut out for. Or perhaps their computer skills are way ahead of yours. Or maybe they have to give a lot of sales presentations and you have very little such experience.

You have to be honest or you've no chance of training yourself up for the job ready for when it comes vacant. But the good news is that almost all these kind of skills are perfectly learnable – even motivating people. Your style might not be the same as someone else's, but it can still be as effective.

So draw up a list of skills you need to learn to be ready for the new challenge when it arrives, and work your way through it learning and practising everything you can. Some skills are easy to read up about, enrol on courses for, or acquire by staying late and practising. But others, of course, will be more difficult. That's where the next stage comes in: talk to your boss.

talk to the boss

What, discuss promotion when there aren't any jobs going? Certainly. Now is the perfect time. You need to let your boss know in plenty of time that you have your eye on promotion in due course. There are two reasons for this:

- If you don't, there's always the danger that when the job finally comes up, your boss will appoint someone from outside without considering you at all. Why? Because they had no idea you were interested in the job. The only way to be sure this doesn't happen is to tell them clearly that you *are* interested before it happens.

- Your boss can tell you better than anyone what skills you would need to acquire to stand a decent chance of getting the job. *And* they can help you acquire them. They can send you on courses, give you extra experience and increase your responsibilities.

Look at it from their point of view. Internal promotions are always easier, cheaper and less disruptive. Next time a suitable job comes up, they'll want to promote from within if they can. So they want to know that when it happens, there's someone in the department who can step into the job. The alternative is finding that not only do they have the upheaval of losing one of their team, but they don't even have anyone else able to fill the gap.

So talk to your boss. This is something you can do at your appraisal, when you discuss your future. Ask them, 'I would like to see myself moving up the career ladder next time an opportunity comes up. What additional skills and experience will I need to be a good candidate for promotion?' Make a note of everything they advise, and ask for their help in acquiring any of these skills that you can't manage on your own. After all, you're adding to your value even before you're promoted so it's in their interests.

internal promotions are always easier, cheaper and less disruptive

caught on the hop

If you get wind of the fact that someone may be leaving before you've had a chance to discuss promotion at your appraisal, ask for a meeting with your boss. Assuming they know that the position may be coming vacant, simply tell them that you would be interested in applying and ask what skills or experience you would need to stand a good chance of success. If they don't know that one of your colleagues is thinking of leaving, and you don't want to break a confidence by telling them, simply say you want to discuss your future with the organisation and have the conversation you would have had at your appraisal.

So your first step is to assess your ability to do the job, identify any weaknesses, and remedy them according to the guidelines set out in the first part of this book. Just as when you are asking for a pay rise you will need to demonstrate:

- a good personal profile
- effective working methods
- good people skills
- creative thinking

… as well as your other more tangible skills, in order to impress your boss and senior managers when you apply for promotion.

demonstrate you can do the job

Whether or not there's a job in the offing at the moment, you want everyone to know that you can do the job you are hoping to move into. You are hoping that when your more senior colleague finally moves on, everyone will assume it's a foregone conclusion that the job's yours. You've seen it happen often enough: everyone can see that the more junior team member is ready-made for the job when it comes up. The closer you can get to that state of affairs, the better.

So how are you going to demonstrate that you can do the job? Essentially by doing it. Always be the first to volunteer if there's any overflow of work being handed down. Put yourself in line for taking over parts of the job – especially taking over responsibilities. If working out the time sheets is an onerous task for your colleague, offer to learn it from them so you can take it over, or at least do part of it. Volunteer to do your colleague's research for them when they write reports. Suggest that if you were trained in using the spreadsheet software, you could enter the day-to-day accounts yourself. And, of course, miss no opportunity to step into as much of the job as necessary when the colleague in question is away on business, on holiday or off sick.

Just one word of caution here: don't get pushy. You'll make yourself unpopular and that won't help your chances of success. You don't want your colleague to think that you are trying to pinch their job. You're not. You want them to stay there until they're ready to move on. It's just that when they *do* move on, you want to be first in line. Some colleagues will actively encourage you and groom you to take over from them when the time comes, while others will feel threatened and nervous if you show any sign of treading on what they see as their territory.

don't break the chain

It doesn't hurt to groom a replacement for yourself. You don't want to miss out on a promotion because your boss can't afford to spare you from the job you're in now. So make sure it doesn't happen: show some other capable person how to do your job, ready to step into your shoes as soon as you get the chance to step out of them.

don't do anything behind their back

If you're dealing with a colleague (or maybe even your boss) whose job you want to train up for and who is easily threatened, you'll need to tread carefully:

- Don't offer to take on too many responsibilities at once. Wait until they have got used to you doing a particular task as a matter of course before adding the next one to your portfolio.

- They won't feel you're closing in if you keep emphasising the gap between the two of you. So point out how, if you take this menial task off their hands, they'll have more time for the really important stuff. For example, 'I can see that the report you're working on is going to be very important to the department. Would you like me to do a bit of running around researching the information for you, so you have more time to invest in the report itself?'

- Don't do anything behind their back. People who are easily threatened can get paranoid. Suppose you decide you want to learn to operate the spreadsheet software, but you're worried that they may feel threatened if you let them know this. So you get someone else to teach you. Now imagine your colleague finds out; what will they think? Not only are you trying to learn their job, but you're trying to do it in secret. So never try this technique – it can backfire horribly.

- If they show any signs of paranoia, tell them what your agenda is. It's perfectly reasonable, and they'd probably do the same themselves. Maybe they already have their eye on someone else's job. Make it very clear that you don't want to replace them until they're ready to move on and up themselves.

you can do better

As well as learning how to do the job in question, look at ways you could improve on it too. Look for opportunities to do even better than the present incumbent, and make a mental note of them. That way, you can make a good strong impression when you apply for the job, by explaining how you see it developing, and again when you finally step into it.

don't blow it at the interview

You may be lucky enough to be offered the job – when it finally comes up – without an interview. But the likelihood is that you won't be the only candidate and your boss will have to invite applications and hold selection interviews.

There is a skill to handling a selection interview, as you know, and one that you'll find plenty of good books on. The important point to make here is that you should handle an internal interview with the same formality and professionalism as you would an interview with any other organisation. You will need to put forward a good, clear case so that your interviewers can compare you on equal terms with any other candidates.

Make absolutely no assumptions about your employers' view of you. They may have overlooked your strong points. There may be managers on the selection panel who don't know you well. Your own manager may have forgotten that you have certain skills or qualifications. They may need reminding that you handled your colleague's job single-handedly when they took that three-week holiday last autumn. Possibly they hadn't realised that the time sheets weren't originally part of your job but that you took over the entire responsibility from your senior colleague six months ago.

The interview is not an informal chat, and the result isn't a foregone conclusion. As with your pay rise, show your employer that you have been adding value to yourself continually, and that you will continue to do so. It's easy for your

make absolutely no assumptions about your employers' view of you

boss to forget that your predecessor was less experienced when they started the job than when they finished, and they may need a gentle reminder that it's OK to grow into a job. So long as you show that you constantly improve, they will feel confident that you can learn quickly to handle the more challenging parts of the job. And help them along further by telling them your ideas for improving on results or systems.

summary

If you want to get promoted, the first thing you need to do is assess your ability to do the job (or all the jobs) you have your eye on. Be honest with yourself, or you restrict your chances of success. And ask your boss for advice on how you could increase your chances of promotion – what skills, experience or qualifications will you need? Whether or not you ask your boss for this advice, you should still let them know that you are keen to be promoted, otherwise you may be overlooked next time the opportunity arises.

Now you need to work on any weak areas in your profile to bring your performance up to the level needed for the job you want to win. This means improving qualifications and technical skills, and also:

- your personal profile
- effective working methods
- good people skills
- creative thinking.

Now demonstrate you can do the job in question by volunteering to take over any excess workload, stand in for your senior colleague when they are away, help them with tasks and so on. (Just make sure you don't tread on any toes.)

When the job finally comes up, apply for it formally and handle the interview process as professionally as you would with an outside organisation. Make no assumptions about what your employers already know about you, but tell them afresh everything that you want them to take into account. And tell them what improvements you feel you could make in the job (without criticising the person who is about to vacate the post).

If you follow these guidelines you have every chance of moving up the organisation as quickly as you deserve to. The faster you climb the career ladder, the more you will be noticed by those above you. This makes it a self-perpetuating process – once you start showing that you have the talent your managers will respond quickly and help you up the ladder.

chapter seventeen

HOW TO FOLLOW UP A BID FOR PROMOTION

Whether or not you get your promotion, you need to know how to respond to the situation. If it's offered, there's a whole new deal to negotiate. And if it's turned down, you still want to salvage something from the exercise and set yourself up for the next opportunity.

... and the pay rise?

If you follow the guidelines in the previous chapter, you have every chance of winning your promotion. And what about the pay rise that goes with it? When you're offered the job, you will almost certainly be offered a pay increase to accompany it. This increase will be negotiable, but let me offer you a word of caution. The pay rise may be well below the level you were hoping for. If this is the case, be prepared to accept it without too much argument. In other words, ask for what you feel you deserve, but set your bottom line lower than you might be tempted to. Your employers may have good reason for believing your salary should be lower than you believe it should be:

- Inevitably, they are taking a gamble moving you into a job with more responsibility than you have been used to.

- You may be expecting the salary your predecessor was on for doing the same job. But your predecessor had experience that you haven't yet gained. They may have started the job on a much lower salary than they left it on, and your employers will equate your value more closely with the starting salary than the leaving salary.

- By promoting you, your boss has automatically given you some degree of pay increase. But they have also transferred you on to a new ladder where your potential has increased considerably: you could end up earning more in this job than you ever could have done in the previous one. This potential for earning more has a value in itself, which you should calculate into your overall compensation package – your boss is certainly taking it into account. And they will know that if they start you too high they will be boosting this potential even further.

once you're in the job your bargaining power will increase

luck or value?

Your boss may take the line that, 'You're lucky to get this new job. Don't push it by asking for too much.' This implication that they are doing you a favour is unfair, so don't stand for it. They offered you this job because it suited *them* to have you do it. If they come out with this line, tell them, 'I thought you offered me this job because I would be valuable to the organisation. Negotiating my salary is a way of establishing what that value is. I believe I will be more valuable than you perhaps think.'

If your salary is negotiated down further than you had hoped in this new job, let your boss know that you intend your pay to increase quickly: 'I recognise that you feel there's an element of risk in appointing anyone new to a job. But I hope that as soon as I've proved my ability to do it we can review my salary with a view to raising it to reflect my value to the company.'

If you are very dissatisfied with the level of pay you're being offered, it is still worth taking the best you can get at this stage. Get your foot in the door (or your feet under the desk) and once you're in the job your bargaining power will increase. But in the meantime you can aim to:

- Agree a specific date for a salary review in, say, four or six months' time.
- Negotiate a performance-related element of your pay.
- Agree a specific rise in response to a specific target. For example, if you successfully resolve the current overtime problems within two months, you will get a specified salary increase from the beginning of July.

All of these options (and you may think of others) are a way of saying that you believe you are worth more than your boss is prepared to commit to. So let them give you a chance to prove your value first, with an undertaking that if you are as good as you promise, you will be rewarded in the relatively short term. The options also give you a justification for seeking a pay rise very soon after your salary has been set.

As well as seeking a salary increase, you also have a chance to renegotiate your whole package. As we've seen before, you might well be able to justify a company car to go with this new job, or a bigger office. And should you get childcare allowance or a better level of health insurance too? Be realistic – ask for what you can justify, as always – but don't miss out on any opportunities for developing the whole package.

If you are being offered substantially less than you clearly feel you deserve, this might at least be a good time to ask your boss to reward you in other ways. If they've just said no to a reasonable request for another £2000 a year, they'll find it that much harder to say no to a car, a home computer or a private office as well.

know where you're going

Make sure you have a detailed meeting with your boss to establish exactly what your objectives are in this new job, and where your priorities should lie. This will enable you to direct your energies towards adding as much value as possible, as quickly as possible. And this, in turn, means you can justify asking for your next pay rise all the sooner.

if the answer is no...

When you ask for a pay rise your boss may agree to everything you're asking for, or to most of it, or to a small percentage, or to none at all. But when it comes to promotion, either you get the job or you don't. Occasionally your employer

get your boss to be as specific as possible

might create a new intermediate post for you (more about that in the next chapter), but generally a no is precisely that. No.

So what do you do? You have the option of leaving, of course, and you might decide to do that if you feel you want to move up the ladder and there's not likely to be another opportunity here for a while. But most people who miss out on promotion still choose to stay in the organisation. Assuming you want to stay – at least for the moment – how do you handle being turned down? There are two important steps you can take to make sure that you still benefit from the situation, even though you haven't got the job you wanted:

- Ask why you weren't appointed to the job.
- Ask for a pay rise.

why didn't you get the job?

Fix up a meeting with your boss, following all the guidelines for asking for a pay rise: preparing your case, and setting up a good half hour to an hour in private with them. Begin by asking for the reasons why you missed out on the promotion. You felt you were a strong candidate, and you'd like to know what your boss considered were your weak points so that you can work on them. That way, you'll stand a better chance next time.

If your boss tries to flannel you, and tell you you're wonderful but the successful candidate was even better, explain that this isn't very helpful: 'I really want to know where I was weak, or where they were stronger than me, so that I can improve my chances next time there's a possibility of promotion. I appreciate that you don't want to hurt my feelings, but you'll be doing me a favour if you give me feedback that helps me in future.'

Get your boss to be as specific as possible about any areas where you may have failed to make the grade:

■ qualifications

■ skills

■ experience

■ interpersonal skills.

Make a written note so you can't forget what they've said, and then make it your mission to work on all these areas ready for the next promotion opportunity. There's no point arguing with your boss about their opinions of you. For one thing, the decision is made now. And for another, if they perceive that you are weak, that's what counts: they make the decisions on promotion. It doesn't matter what you think.

If your boss has, say, three reasons for not promoting you yet and you argue defensively and vociferously with the first one, they may decide not to bother to mention the others and thus save themselves an unpleasant row. Few people enjoy criticising others, so make it easy for them. Otherwise you may never find out all the things you need to know to improve your chances next time.

swallow your pride

Whatever happens, make sure you are pleasant and co-operative with the person who gets the job you wanted, even if you now have to work directly under them. They may be a previous colleague or some-one from outside the organisation. Either way, by taking the job, they only did what you would have done yourself in their position. No mat-ter how strongly you believe they are the wrong person for the job, if you behave badly towards them in any way, you will be seen as petty and mean-spirited. This image will do nothing for your chances of promotion, salary increase or anything else in the future. Be mag-nanimous, however, and you'll score big brownie points.

ask for a pay rise

You've just gone through the whole process of demonstrating your value in order to earn the promotion. You may have missed out there, but you've almost certainly shown that you are at least some way better than the job you're doing. So capitalise on this opportunity to get your salary increased, according to all the principles we've already covered.

And let's not forget that you have the psychological advantage here. I'm not suggesting you ask for a rise you don't deserve, but there's no denying that this is good timing. Your boss has already turned you down for promotion. They're going to feel dreadful if they don't even give you a pay rise in compensation. Of course, they may be prepared to feel dreadful. But if you've got a strong case for a rise, it would take a pretty hard-headed boss to refuse you just now.

no chance?

And what if there's no chance for promotion? Maybe you work for a small company, or in a 'flat' organisation. Or perhaps it's just that no one above you shows any sign of leaving, so the opportunity doesn't arise. If this happens, don't despair. You simply need to create a new job for yourself and make sure you get the salary and the job title that reflects the added responsibilities and achievements. And that's what the next chapter is all about.

summary

Whether or not you get the job, you'll need to make the right response. If you are offered it:

- Negotiate the best overall deal you can.
- Be prepared to set your bottom line lower than you normally would.
- Set in place an arrangement that ensures that if you prove your value, you will get a salary increase within the next few months.

If the answer is no:

- Ask why you didn't get the job, and get your boss to be specific.
- Ask for a pay rise.

18

HOW TO CREATE A JOB FOR YOURSELF

What do you do if you're itching for promotion and there's nowhere to go? No one above you is showing any signs of moving, or maybe there aren't many people above you because the organisation has flattened its management structure. Or maybe there's one job that might come up, but ten other talented people with more experience than you will all be after it.

The answer (as you'll have guessed from the chapter title) is to create a new job for yourself. Effectively you promote yourself, and then encourage your boss to join in. There are plenty of ways you can do this and, with a bit of creative thought, you should find at least one approach that will work for you.

extend your skills sideways

We've already looked at the option of extending your skills to undertake a senior colleague or boss's work if you have your eye on their job. But this is a bit different. The aim here is to extend your skills so that you can do – or at least help out with – the work of colleagues at your level. So if you work in customer accounts, learn how to handle some of the work of the bought ledger. If you work in PR and you mostly organise events while your colleague handles press relations, learn how to deal with the press too.

And what's the point of that, you may ask? The point is that it makes you more valuable to the organisation. You can cover when your colleague is off sick or on leave, or simply help out when their workload becomes excessive. You'll be invaluable in an emergency. In the short term, of course, this means you're worth a salary increase at the least. But we're talking about promotion here. So how does it help you get promoted? Let me give you a couple of examples:

- Your employers decide to create a new layer of management within your department. Who is the person who knows a fair amount about every job – at least enough to oversee them? You are.

- Your colleague leaves. You point out to your boss that you can handle their job as well as your own, so long as you have an assistant. That way, they'll

never miss a chance
to volunteer

have two people in place who both know the ropes – and you've just effectively moved up a rung with an assistant working for you.

The simplest way to learn new skills is to ask. Tell your boss, 'I'd like to learn how to run the bought ledger accounts. If I gave up a few lunch hours, could I sit with Emily and learn it from her?' Your boss is hardly likely to refuse, and you can point out that it will make emergency cover easier to organise in future.

don't waste time

It is far more useful to learn new skills or take on extra responsibilities than simply to work longer hours. In fact, people who work long hours are often taken for granted and go unrecognised. The aim here is not simply to make yourself more valuable, but to make yourself more senior. To do that, any extra hours should be invested in broadening your skills, not simply using those you already have.

increase your responsibilities

Quite apart from adding to your skills, you also need to keep increasing your responsibilities at every opportunity. It is the level of responsibility you carry that really determines your seniority. So never miss a chance to volunteer: 'I can do that' should be constantly on the tip of your tongue. Offer to take over negotiating with suppliers, or volunteer to handle all the administration for trade shows – booking the stands, organising the printers, making hotel reservations, and so on.

And how does this help when there's no job available to move up into? What you have to do is this. Once these new responsibilities have become established as part of your job, ask for a meeting with your boss. Explain that you feel your job title no longer reflects the job you're really doing. You're not so much a PR assistant as a PR administrator. You've added a great deal of value to the job you do, and you'd appreciate a change in job title to reflect and reward this.

You haven't asked for a promotion, but a change in job title to something more senior is a *de facto* promotion. You may also want to ask for a pay rise at the same time. This is rather up to your own judgement. You might ask for a better job title as part of a salary review – perhaps in exchange for conceding a proportion of the rise you're asking for. But you can equally well make this an isolated request. If you don't feel you can justify asking for a pay rise at this stage, you can still ask for a better job title.

Once the job title is established, you can build on it. Next time you can demonstrate a substantial increase in value you can ask for a pay rise, and you can point out that your remuneration is well below average for a PR administrator.

carve a niche for yourself

This technique works extremely well in relatively small companies, as well as in larger ones. What you have to do is identify a job that doesn't exist and then groom yourself for it. For example, if you're in marketing and experienced at giving presentations, you might have a word with your boss and say, 'Jake is turning into a very promising presenter. Would it be helpful if I took him aside and gave him a few additional pointers? It wouldn't be difficult to turn him into a really strong asset to the department.'

Once you've improved Jake's performance, you offer to do the same for Belinda and Amin too. That goes well, so you offer to take Jake along with you to the next trade show so he can learn to man an exhibition stand effectively. Before long, you go to your boss and say, 'I've noticed the company training manual is a bit out of date. Would it help if I drafted some rewrites?'

top news

If you're looking for a new role to take on, launching an internal newsletter can be a particularly useful one. If you work for a large organisation that already has a staff newsletter, perhaps you could start one for your particular branch. A newsletter – followed by taking on a few other strategic responsibilities – can lead your job to meta-morphose into communications, HR or public relations. What's more, it gives you a high profile in the wider organisation so that other managers and more senior executives get to know you. This sort of networking makes you more visible and is really useful for future pay rises and promotions.

You can see what's happening here: you're becoming the training manager for the section or even the whole company. If your boss doesn't notice this, you point it out to them in due course (once your boss has started relying on your expertise as a trainer). There are two ways of doing this:

- Tell your boss you think the company needs a training manager. Write a proposal outlining what you believe the job should entail, and what the benefit would be to the organisation. When you have persuaded your boss to create the post, apply for it yourself. You are in a stronger position than anyone else to do the job.

- Ask for a meeting with your boss. Point out that you are thoroughly enjoying the challenge of taking on the training, and you feel you're valuable to the company. Tell them you would like to change your job remit to include the role of training manager officially. This will inevitably involve some kind of promotion, if only because your job title will improve – which as we've already seen constitutes a promotion in effect.

There are plenty of niches you can create for yourself. In a small organisation, PR is often a good one. Training is another, as is software manager. You could

personal bonds ... are very important to companies

offer to set up a website for the company, and end up as IT manager. There's rarely a shortage of jobs you can create; it's simply a matter of looking for a gap in the organisation that matches your skills.

specialise in relationships

Another way in which you can boost your chances of promotion into a job that doesn't yet exist is by building really strong relationships with the people you work with. Suppose you work with suppliers. You are responsible for negotiating some terrific deals, which save the company money. At the same time, you make sure that the suppliers are paid really promptly and that orders are processed well in advance, making their workload far easier to plan. The suppliers love you, and are really keen to deal with you personally whenever difficulties arise or new deals need negotiating.

It won't take much for your boss to realise that you are a great asset to the organisation, and would be very hard to replace. These kind of personal bonds, or special relationships, are very important to companies. Once you have strengthened your position in this way, you can talk to your boss about a change of job title, as we saw earlier. After all you're no longer just a buying assistant – you're the only buyer that will do for these suppliers. So shouldn't you at least become a junior buying manager, or a buying executive, or the buyer for the Midlands?

You can adopt exactly the same approach to building indispensable relationships with customers, or with other staff or managers in the organisation. It is far harder to replace someone whose skills lie in personal relationships than one whose value lies in a technical ability such as book keeping or computer skills. Your boss knows this, so you have a great deal of bargaining power.

summary

Just because you can't see a job in your organisation that you could move up into in the near future, it doesn't mean you have no chance of promotion. You'll just have to create your own job, that's all. There are four classic ways to do this:

- *Extend your skills sideways*, ready to be the best candidate for any new job that is created.

- *Increase your responsibilities*. If this doesn't lead to promotion, ask for a new job title to reflect the work you now do. Ask for a pay rise to go with it. Later on, ask for an assistant to help you with the workload. That looks like promotion to me.

- *Carve a niche for yourself*. Identify a job that doesn't exist in your organisation and then groom yourself for it.

- *Specialise in relationships*. Become so important and valuable to customers, suppliers or other managers in the company, that you have sufficient bargaining power to negotiate for a change in job title, a pay rise and so on. In other words, a *de facto* promotion.

chapter nineteen

HOW TO KNOW WHEN IT'S TIME TO GO

When your boss refuses to give you the pay rise or promotion you feel you deserve, it's very tempting to tell them to stick their job. You'll go and find another employer who appreciates you and knows how to show it. And there are times when this really is the best decision. But there are several factors you would be wise to consider before you hand in your notice.

There is inevitably a risk in deciding to change jobs, and whether it is worth taking that risk depends on a host of things, including your present job, your new job (if you take one) and yourself. So let's consider each in turn.

play it cool

If you do decide to leave, there's nothing to gain by telling your present employer just what you think of them. Far better to stay on pleasant terms. Sure, you can tell them politely why you've decided you can do better elsewhere, but don't get on the wrong side of them. You might need a reference from them and, even if you don't, you don't want people around saying things that will damage your reputation. One of your bosses may even end up working with you again one day. So once you've got what you want, keep the moral high ground and resist the urge to say how you really feel.

your present job

Are you really deeply fed up with the job, or is this just a short-term reaction to not getting the pay rise or promotion you want? If the dissatisfaction goes deep, it may well be time to change. If, for example, you don't get on with the people, or you find the organisation over-political or excessively bureaucratic and inflexible, this is probably a long-term problem that won't go away until you leave the job.

But it may be that your frustration is relatively recent, and mostly to do with pay or promotion. In that case, it's worth thinking about the prevailing charac-

remember that no organisation is perfect

ter of the company. Are they always poor payers, or slow to promote talent, or have you just hit a temporary blip? Is this a problem that would evaporate if your boss moved on, perhaps (and if so, how likely is this to happen)? Or might things resolve if you get that job you're after when a particular colleague leaves in another six months or so?

Broadly speaking, if your desire to leave is the result of some relatively recent development such as being passed over for promotion, it's a good idea to wait for a while before making a decision on whether to leave. But if you've been unhappy in the job for some time, leaving is more likely to be the right decision. So think about the real reasons you want to go before you rush into anything.

Remember that no organisation is perfect, and you shouldn't balance up your knowledge of your present company with an imaginary perfect employer, because that's not where you'll end up. Does your employer really pay less than other companies? If so, are there other compensating factors you should take into account? For example, does your employer offer more stimulating work challenges, or longer holidays?

no risk-free guarantee

Bear in mind that staying where you are isn't necessarily the safe option. There is risk in everything, after all. If you've been there more than five or six years, a decision to stay could ultimately lead to you looking less employable to other organisations in the future – you'll begin to look inexperienced in taking on new challenges. And if pay or promotion really is poor where you are now, you risk losing the opportunity to earn more and climb the ladder faster.

there must be some good things about your present job

the new job

Suppose you leave, and find that the new job isn't all you'd hoped. How much would you regret the decision? Would you feel you were no worse off, or would you be really upset? Talk to other people in the industry, and to any prospective employers, and make sure that pay and promotion prospects are genuinely better than they are with your present employer.

No matter how fed up you are at the moment, there must be some good things about your present job. So sit down and think them through. Make a note of the good things you really wouldn't want to give up. They might include:

- Working with people you like.
- Plenty of challenges.
- Lots of variety.
- Convenient location.
- Good promotion prospects (even if pay is poor).
- Good salary (even if promotion prospects are sparse).
- Your ideas are listened to.
- Flexible hours.
- A boss you get on well with.
- The chance to add plenty of skills to your portfolio.
- Specific skills – maybe you get to give plenty of presentations which you enjoy, or you get involved in training other people. Sometimes an ostensibly equivalent job in another organisation would mean spending your time on a very different balance of tasks.

Once you've identified what is important to you at work, you can find out how any new employer would score on these factors. You don't want to leave an employer who pays badly to join one who pays you well but at the cost of working with people you don't get on with, with no challenge and far less opportunity to organise events or influence systems or whatever else it is you enjoy at the moment.

yourself

And how about you? Your personal situation is important. You may need more money at the moment to cover your living expenses, in which case staying where you are is not a good prospect if your employer won't give you a rise. On the other hand, how confident are you that your new job will work out? And if it didn't, would you still be able to find another job that would pay what you need? Is there a greater danger of redundancy if you move (or, indeed, if you stay)? Would there be hidden costs if you changed jobs, such as higher travelling costs, or less opportunity for overtime or bonuses?

Your financial security is probably important (although more so for some of us than others). But there are other factors, too. How well does your present job fit with your personal life, and how would a new job compare? Here are a few examples (some of which overlap with the list of good points you've already made):

- Convenient location.
- Good arrangements for personal time off (for the dentist, or waiting for a washing machine to be delivered).
- You're able to work from home sometimes.
- Hours fit in with dropping kids at school, playing squash or football regularly, missing the rush hour or whatever else.
- Holidays fit in conveniently.
- You can socialise with your colleagues after work.

... And so on.

Some of us would rather have the convenience than the extra money, and that's fine. If so, take these factors into account before you rush into another job that will pay better but that will cause havoc in your home life.

study the field

Of course, it's tough when you don't know exactly what you can expect from another employer. But at this stage you're only making a decision in principle on whether to go. Talking to friends and ex-colleagues in other organisations of any kind will tell you broadly what current trends are in holiday entitlements, personal time off or working from home. If the companies they have experience of happen to be in your industry, that's a bonus. But ask around as much as you can to find out whether your personal priorities are easy to find or whether lighting upon another employer as convenient as yours is going to take a long search.

deciding to go

When you have balanced up all these factors, you will know whether you want to leave or not. Assuming you decide that you do, remember that you don't have to make the final decision until you have a job to go to. You can test the water first by applying for other jobs and seeing how employable you are.

As we've already seen, however, don't call your boss's bluff by telling them you've got a job offer you're going to take if they don't give you the pay rise you want. Never tell them you're leaving unless you really are. If they respond by making you a better offer, well, then you can reconsider. But don't ask them to do it, and don't ever count on them fighting to keep you.

If you're leaving because the money you're getting isn't up to what you deserve, you'll be looking for a job that pays more than you earn now. Depending on the offer you're made, this might well mean negotiating with your

don't ever count on them fighting to keep you

prospective employer. Follow the rules for negotiating that we've already covered and, if the new job is a step up, incorporate the guidelines for negotiating a pay rise that goes with a promotion.

It is crucial that you decide what your bottom line is. It's easy to be tempted into a new job by the flattery of being offered it, and a lot of us find it difficult to say no. But if the job doesn't offer a better deal than you're getting now, don't take it. Having said that, take into account the overall deal – including personal and motivational factors – and not only the financial package.

Whatever you do, don't hand in your notice until you have a written job offer in your hand, stating terms that you are happy with. If your boss is likely to hold it against you that you're looking for another job, don't let them get wind of it until you have that firm, written guarantee. Wait until all the negotiations are finished, and then hand in your notice.

a written guarantee

To a new employer, you're an unknown quantity. They may understandably want to wait until they see what you're worth before they pay you accordingly. Often, a new employer will offer you a starting salary with a promise that if you complete your probationary period your pay will go up. Unless you get this in writing, specifying the amount of the rise, don't count on it. Many employers are reliable, but you don't know these people that well yet. If they won't put it in writing, you should ask yourself (and indeed them) why not.

summary

Sometimes you reach the point when it's time to leave your present job and find a more suitable employer. But before you make a decision that will affect your whole life, consider the pros and cons of going in terms of:

■ your present job

■ the new job

■ yourself.

If you still feel that the best decision is to go, find a new job first, negotiate a deal, then tell your employer.

And remember, once you arrive in your new job, you're back in the same position all over again. Keep following all the guidelines in the first part of this book to make sure that you constantly add value to yourself, so you can justify pay rises and promotions – or whatever it is you want – with your new employer. No matter how good a starting salary you negotiate, remember it's in your boss's interests to keep rewarding good performance so that you remain motivated to keep improving. Do them a favour: practise all the skills you've been learning in this book – from adding value to negotiating effectively – and show them how it's done.